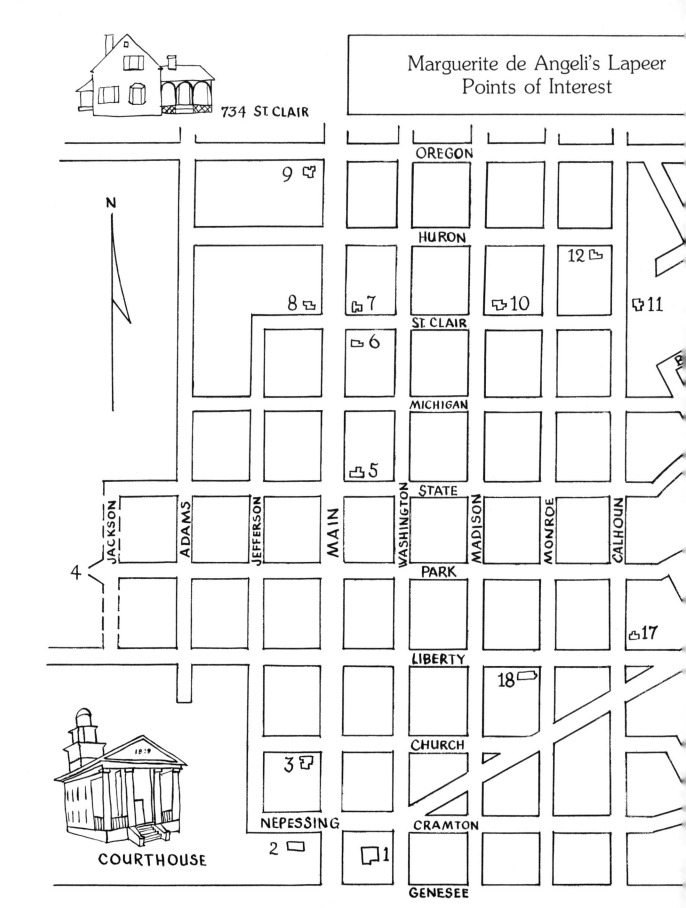

734 ST. CLAIR

Marguerite de Angeli's Lapeer
Points of Interest

N

OREGON

9

HURON

12

8   7

10   11

ST. CLAIR

6

MICHIGAN

5

STATE

JACKSON   ADAMS   JEFFERSON   MAIN   WASHINGTON   MADISON   MONROE   CALHOUN

4

PARK

17

LIBERTY

18

CHURCH

3

COURTHOUSE   NEPESSING   CRAMTON

2   1

GENESEE

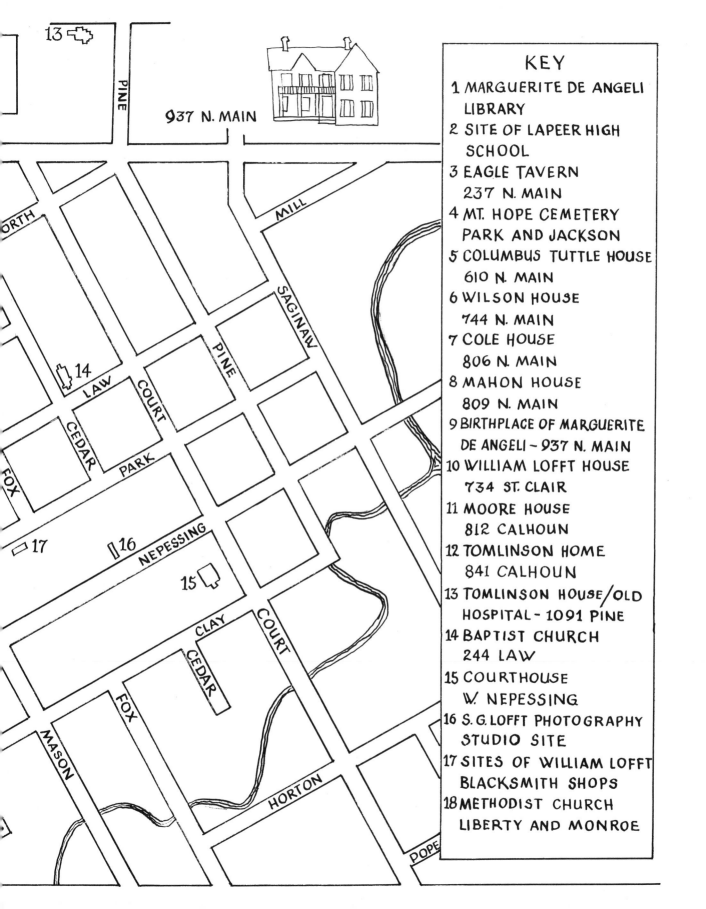

937 N. MAIN

KEY

1. MARGUERITE DE ANGELI LIBRARY
2. SITE OF LAPEER HIGH SCHOOL
3. EAGLE TAVERN 237 N. MAIN
4. MT. HOPE CEMETERY PARK AND JACKSON
5. COLUMBUS TUTTLE HOUSE 610 N. MAIN
6. WILSON HOUSE 744 N. MAIN
7. COLE HOUSE 806 N. MAIN
8. MAHON HOUSE 809 N. MAIN
9. BIRTHPLACE OF MARGUERITE DE ANGELI - 937 N. MAIN
10. WILLIAM LOFFT HOUSE 734 ST. CLAIR
11. MOORE HOUSE 812 CALHOUN
12. TOMLINSON HOME 841 CALHOUN
13. TOMLINSON HOUSE/OLD HOSPITAL - 1091 PINE
14. BAPTIST CHURCH 244 LAW
15. COURTHOUSE W. NEPESSING
16. S. G. LOFFT PHOTOGRAPHY STUDIO SITE
17. SITES OF WILLIAM LOFFT BLACKSMITH SHOPS
18. METHODIST CHURCH LIBERTY AND MONROE

MARGUERITE DE ANGELI'S
LAPEER POINTS OF INTEREST

KEY TO MAP

1. The Marguerite de Angeli Library at 921 W. Nepessing contains exhibits of the author's manuscripts, art-works, books and memorabilia.

2. Originally built by the White family as a possible court house, the building became Lapeer High School. It was here that the calf was tied in the belfry, as described in *Copper-Toed Boots*. The school was razed in 1965 and the Administration Building of the Lapeer Schools now occupies the spot.

3. Eagle Tavern at 237 N. Main was built in 1839. It was the home of the E.T. White family from 1920-1979.

4. Mt. Hope Cemetery's main gates were wrought by William Lofft in his Lapeer blacksmith shop. Graves of the Loffts and Tuttles are located in the cemetery.

5. Columbus Tuttle House at 610 N. Main was built in 1872 in Queen Anne style. Home of Marguerite's mother and family. The attic of this house was featured in *Ted and Nina Have a Happy Rainy Day*.

6. Wilson House at 744 N. Main was a girlhood home of Marguerite Lofft.

7. Cole House at 806 N. Main was the home of the Lofft family in 1901.

8. The Mahon House at 809 N. Main is another early home of Marguerite and her family.

9. De Angeli Birthplace at 937 N. Main was built in the early 1880s. A plaque marking Marguerite's March 14, 1889 birthplace was erected in 1971.

10. The Lofft Home at 734 St. Clair was featured in *Copper-Toed Boots*. It was home for the family from circa 1870 until 1927.

11. Moore House at 812 Calhoun was a favorite home of Marguerite Lofft when she lived there, circa 1896.

12. Samuel Tomlinson home at 841 Calhoun was mentioned in *Copper-Toed Boots*. This is the former home of Ash, Shad's friend.

13. The later home of the Tomlinsons is still located at 1091 Pine. It served as Lapeer's hospital for many years.

14. The original Baptist church building is now the Henley Recreation Center. The Tuttle family held membership there, and Marguerite attended as a child.

15. The 1839 Court House was pictured and mentioned in *Copper-Toed Boots*. Historical displays are now housed there.

16. The Shad Lofft photography studio was located above the long-time Zemmer Drug Store (now Perry's).

17. William Lofft's blacksmith shops in Lapeer were located where Baird-Newton's parking lot is now located, and in the area behind the Lyric Mall.

18. The 1896 Methodist church building was where the Loffts were active. Marguerite sang here on a visit to Lapeer in the early 1900s.

Original in de Angeli Library, Lapeer.

Marguerite de Angeli's Children's Book Week Poster for 1948.

MICHIGAN'S MARGUERITE DE ANGELI

The Story of Lapeer's Native
Author-Illustrator

by William Anderson

Marguerite de Angeli Library
Lapeer, Michigan

This activity is supported by the Michigan Council for the Arts through their Regional V Regranting Agency - The Greater Flint Arts Council

ACKNOWLEDGEMENTS

This book is the result of Lapeer, Michigan's pride in claiming one of this century's foremost creators of children's books, Marguerite de Angeli. It stems from the Lapeer County Historical Society and the Marguerite de Angeli Library's dedication in preserving this literary heritage.

Compiling resource material which led to *Michigan's Marguerite de Angeli* is the result of input from many sources. Thanks go to Mrs. de Angeli herself, for her visit to this writer's classroom, and correspondence relating to her life in Lapeer and her work as author-artist. Appreciated is the assistance of the author's family: her son Arthur of Florida, her granddaughter Kate Creitz of Troy, and her brother, Mr. Harry Lofft. Adelle Walton, Marguerite's niece, has provided information and photos. In Lapeer, Marguerite de Angeli's cousin Ruth Turnbull has assisted with history and memory.

The staff at the Marguerite de Angeli Library in Lapeer made its large collection of memorabilia available for research and study. Also useful were the historical collections of the Lapeer County Historical Society. At Central Michigan University, the Clarke Historical Library was helpful in making its de Angeli collection available. Carolyn Field, formerly of the Free Library of Philadelphia, has offered a long and helpful assistance. In Lapeer, the assistance of Dr. Jean Liming of the Lapeer Community Schools was valuable.

The Michigan Council for the Arts assisted in funding publication of this volume, and Webco Press aided in the printing.

The majority of the historic photos and art-works reproduced herein are from originals now preserved at the de Angeli Library in Lapeer. Betty Spaulding of Lapeer designed the map of historic sites which pertain to our local author. Art from books by Mrs. de Angeli appears through courtesy of the Doubleday Company.

"This book is dedicated to all Children Everywhere and Always", reads Marguerite de Angeli's talisman for her *Book of Nursery and Mother Goose Rhymes. This* book is dedicated to all children and former children who have appreciated Marguerite de Angeli's wonderful story-telling and outstanding illustrating abilities, and who want to know more about her connection with her hometown of Lapeer.

W.T.A.
March 14, 1987

INTRODUCTION

For nearly a century, Lapeer, Michigan has known Marguerite Lofft de Angeli.

Today, memories of her 1890's childhood spent in the small Michigan town as the daughter of the local photographer and granddaughter of the village blacksmith remain only in her own prose. No one is left to remember the enthusiastic girl who sketched on blank pages of books and embellished the wallpaper with imaginative designs. Of all the contemporaries of her Lapeer girlhood, Marguerite alone remains.

A few old-timers still recall Marguerite de Angeli as a young bride, returning from Philadelphia to visit her relatives just before World War I. She was still well acquainted then; 1902, the year her family had moved to Pennsylvania, was not so far in the past when Marguerite came to visit in 1912. It is recalled that the young matron often had an infant in tow when she came to visit her grandparents, her aunts, uncles and cousins; eventually, she had six children. Even then, with her pre-school children, the family noted that Marguerite was determined to study art. While living in Detroit with her husband John Dailey de Angeli and the enlarging family, she managed to squeeze in art classes between home duties and her burgeoning career as a concert contralto. That era, and her continuing pleasure in returning to Lapeer, is carefully chronicled in her autobiography, *Butter at the Old Price.*

Old friends and remaining family in Lapeer were pleased, but not astonished when they started seeing Marguerite de Angeli's illustrations in the pages of *The Country Gentleman* and other popular magazines. And no one in town was surprised when, during the Depression, Marguerite began writing her own books for children and illustrating them. When she started her career as an author in 1935, she possessed the credentials she needed — with five children of her own and a carefully honed artist's eye.

But interest became keen when people learned that Marguerite de Angeli published a book about Lapeer as it was in the 1870s. When *Copper-Toed Boots* appeared in 1938, bonds with home were permanently strengthened. Although Philadelphia had claimed her for years, *Copper-Toed Boots* made her a Lapeer heroine.

Throughout her fifty-year career as author-illustrator, Marguerite de Angeli's hometown watched with pride as her work and her fame accumulated. Finally, there were thirty books bearing her name, dozens of books with her illustrations, and at least as many prestigious awards, honors and recognitions.

And Marguerite de Angeli kept coming home. When she traveled to Cleveland to accept the 1950 Newbery medal — the Pulitzer of children's publishing — she stopped in Lapeer to share her honor. When the Regina Award was given her for lasting contributions to children's books in 1968, Marguerite brought the silver medallion to Lapeer to share before returning to Philadelphia. Both of the medals — previewed at the Lapeer library by the author when they were freshly received — now occupy places of honor in the Marguerite de Angeli Library in Lapeer today.

Her Lapeer visits became a tradition, and while the author was celebrating her ninetieth birthday year in 1979, Marguerite was once again drawn to her birthplace. And the road led back again in 1981, when the Lapeer City Library became the Marguerite de Angeli Library. She watched, along with hundreds of her admirers gathered on the library lawn, as the old sign came down and the new sign bearing her name appeared over the door.

Well into her nineties then, but again a newly-published author with her final book, Marguerite de Angeli referred to the library re-dedication as "one of the happiest days of my life."

"It means a great deal to me to know that I am loved in Lapeer," Marguerite de Angeli said. That long love for her Michigan roots has been nurtured in books, in illustrations, and in person, as generations of readers in Lapeer grow up knowing that someone special is from their town.

The roots of this pioneer in children's publishing and her connection with her mid-Michigan birthplace reach back even farther than her March 14, 1889 birthdate. Marguerite de Angeli's family was present when Lapeer was a young settlement being carved from the forest and traces of the Loffts and Tuttles are still evident today. This book will chronicle the long and enduring link that has made the world-famous writer and artist Lapeer's own Marguerite de Angeli.

I. LAPEER ROOTS AND RELATIVES

Marguerite de Angeli's earliest concrete memories of her life in Lapeer, Michigan include "large family gatherings at which there might be as many as forty-five people, excellent food and much laughter." That feeling of family, that sense of being "surrounded by love and affection, the most essential needs of my life" was a quality that enlivened Marguerite de Angeli's life and infused her writings. And the setting for her girlhood in Lapeer was one that teemed with family...Loffts and Lockwoods, Tuttles, Turnbulls and Houghs.

Her family had been among the early pioneers of Lapeer. Although they did not stretch back as far as the Whites and the Harts, who had founded the town in 1831, Marguerite's maternal grandparents, Columbus and Eunice Tuttle had arrived in Lapeer County in 1853, and her father's parents, William and Maggie Lofft, came to live in the county seat town in 1862. Both her parents, Ruby Tuttle and Shad Lofft, were reared in the growing community, married there and started a family in their hometown.

"Michigan fever" had brought settlers--mainly New Englanders--to the heavily wooded region which could be reached by a three-day stagecoach ride north from Pontiac. As Marguerite de Angeli describes it, "...there was nothing there but a wilderness, and Michigan wasn't even a state. It was good farming land and there was plenty of wood for the cutting." Indeed, remnants of those awesome forests remained intact even during Marguerite's childhood sixty years later. "There were still stump fences confining the fields" she recalled, "tremendous ten-foot high stumps standing on edge with roots interlaced. What trees must have sprung from such roots!"

Lumbering and then farming dominated the early years of Lapeer's history. Both sides of Marguerite's family directly were connected with the town's prime industries: the Tuttles, operating a sawmill, a door, sash and blind factory and William Lofft, the British-born blacksmith, who for over fifty years worked with iron and forged horseshoes "and fitted them to great farm horses with backs as broad as Ma's kitchen table."

THE LOFFTS

Marguerite de Angeli always relished the stories told by her Grandfather Lofft as the family sat under the summer stars on the porch of his home on St. Clair Street in Lapeer. In his British diction, William Lofft told of generations of family who forged giant ship anchors at Sheerness, Isle of Sheppy, a town at the mouth of the Thames River in England.

William Wise Lofft was born at Sheerness on September 27, 1837, but he spent most of his long life in Lapeer, well-known and loved as the town blacksmith. He was a mechanical man, a constant reader, a staunch Methodist, a singer and a commendable penman. Among the relics of his family now displayed at the Marguerite de Angeli Library in Lapeer is a composition book penned by William Lofft as a student in England. His ornate, spidery handwriting fills the pages, along with solutions to mathematics problems like this one:

"A gentleman has an annuity of 89 pounds, 17 shillings per annum. I desire to know how much he may spend daily, that at year's end he may lay up 200 guineas, and give to the poor quarterly 10 Moidores?"

The Lofft home in 1934

He was served well by his knowledge of business through his many years in Lapeer. William Lofft became a fine cabinet-maker, but his life's work was that of a blacksmith. Early in life, he decided to follow the family tradition as a smith. He was indentured as an apprentice blacksmith; his document of indenture, like his composition book, crossed the Atlantic with him when Lofft came to America. It was treasured by his family as a link with origins in Great Britain, and it is treasured in Lapeer today.

When he was twenty, in 1857, the Lofft family--parents, brothers and sisters--emigrated to Canada. They settled at Goderich, where William found work at his trade. On September 6, 1862, he married Margaret J. Sloan.

Maggie Sloan was four years younger than her husband; she was born at Goderich in 1841. In the spring of 1863, William and Maggie Lofft came to Lapeer, joining the influx of Canadians who were lured to Michigan by the thriving lumbering-based economy.* There were over 2,000 people living in Lapeer when the Loffts arrived to settle. It appeared to be a promising place and "there was plenty of work for a smith but not much money," according to *Copper-Toed Boots*. In Lapeer, Lofft worked as a smith for two years before opening his own business.

"How I would love to visit my grandfather's shop!" exclaimed Marguerite de Angeli on one of her visits to Lapeer. Obviously, the blacksmith shop was a place of enchantment for children, with the sparks flying, the giant bellows, the clanging of hammer with the anvil and the horses being fitted with their iron shoes. Today, the question is, "Where did the Lofft shop stand in Lapeer?"

Harry Lofft, Marguerite's brother, believes that the shop was in several locations. This is reasonable, for Mr. Lofft was a fixture downtown for nearly sixty years, and his shop could have changed locations a number of times. Harry thinks that the first shop was south of the Court House. All evidence points to the later establishments being in the area north of Nepessing Street, most specifically, where the parking lot now exists. With urban development, the old buildings vanished in favor of parking places behind the Lyric Mall and beyond. At that time, the precise spot of the Lofft locale disappeared.

Several pieces of evidence pinpoint approximations of the smithy's shop. One is the 1876 advertisement in *The Weekly Clarion* which directs customers to the Lofft establishment "near the Presbyterian church". Referring to the 1874 *Atlas of Lapeer County*, there is indeed a "BS. S." on the east side of Calhoun Street, directly opposite the church. This would have been the shop site at the time described in *Copper-Toed Boots*. The present Baird-Newton parking lot occupies the site now.

William Lofft, Lapeer's blacksmith, around 1894

Most of the Sloans also moved to Michigan. James Sloan, Maggie's father, died in Lapeer in 1889 and is buried in the town's Mt. Hope Cemetery, along with her brother William and sisters Kate and Sue. The Loffts are buried close by.

The 1884 *History of Lapeer County* mentions Lofft's "present location on Fox Street". The city map also indicates a blacksmith shop next to the City Livery on Fox, so apparently William Lofft took over that spot. Ruth Turnbull of Lapeer has suggested that the shop location must have been within the parking lot area behind the Lyric Mall. Doubtlessly the building vanished years ago, as Harry Lofft recalls it as simply a large shed, with doors on the front.

Since the Lofft shop was likely on rented downtown property, it does not show as a named site on city maps. But easily identified is the Lofft home, the setting for *Copper-Toed Boots*, which Marguerite de Angeli describes and depicts with graphic detail in her book. About five blocks from his shop location, at the corner of St. Clair and Madison Streets, William and Maggie Lofft established their long-time home in Lapeer. Because William was a good carpenter, it seems likely that he did much of the work building the home, and through the years, it has changed little since its construction around 1870 or before. The story-and-a-half house was portrayed as the endpapers of *Copper-Toed Boots* (and is used on the cover of this book) in a color illustration by Marguerite. She claimed she avoided looking at photos of the house, because she felt that "if you draw from memory, you get something into the picture that you would not get from a photograph...there's a feeling, there's an atmosphere about it that you get." The ultimate compliment was paid Marguerite when her mother exclaimed when she saw her daughter's work, "I don't see how you remembered it this well, because that's the way it looked!"

The Loffts' first-born child was William Samuel, who arrived in 1863, and their second son, Shadrach George, was born on March 22, 1865.

Work and home and church seemed to summarize the lives of William and Maggie Lofft in Lapeer. Their involvement with the Methodist church in town is well chronicled. On arrival in Lapeer, the Loffts had become active with the building project of the 1865 Methodist church building on Monroe Street. Maggie worked in the women's church circles, providing food for socials and working on projects to raise money for the building of both the 1865 and 1895 church structures. She held meetings of the W.F.M.S. at the Lofft home on St. Clair and participated with the Ladies Aid.

While Maggie was active in church work, William Lofft was very much a cornerstone of the Methodist church. He was musical, and could sing most any part needed in the choir and the Philharmonics male quartet. Together, William Lofft served the Methodists musically for over 50 years, many of those years as music director. Church records reveal that he was prominent in many capacities, including church steward, Sabbath school leader and that "he contributed a great many solos". At both the 1865 and 1896 building dedication services, Mr. Lofft participated musically. Shad Vincent, Lapeer's pioneer druggist, led the Philharmonic Society and William Lofft performed often with the ensemble that was easily the town's leading musical group. After Mr. Vincent decamped to the Episcopalians, Mr. Lofft filled the leadership role. He was often called on to perform and speak, and bridged the past at the Farewell services for the old Methodist church building in 1896 by describing the dedication of the 1865 facility.

In addition to his good diction and speaking delivery, Mr. Lofft was meticulous in his appearance on such occasions. On Sundays, he traded his leather blacksmith's apron for, as his granddaughter Marguerite recalled, "the proper long-tailed coat and striped trousers, wing collar and white tie." Once, on a visit to Lapeer from Philadelphia, Marguerite sang a duet with her grandfather at the Methodist Church. She was surprised to see tears streaming down his cheeks as they harmonized on "O Perfect Love."

Will Lofft, the oldest son, married Marjorie Belkap and settled in Detroit. Will worked

An ad for the blacksmith shop, 1876

The Lofft home at 734 St. Clair, as it appears today.

Maggie Lofft, (second row, left), posed with a number of early Lapeer women, circa 1890. Others identified are: Top row: Mrs. Vansciever, ?, Mrs. Vail, Mrs. Barber, and Mrs. Anstead. Second row, next to Mrs. Lofft: Mrs. Vosburgh, ?, Bottom: ?, ?, Mrs. Gray.

William and Maggie Lofft at their golden wedding celebration in Lapeer, 1912.

*"Pa was making a pair of gates for the new cemetery. Shad thought they were wonderful...when Pa made things like the cemetery gates, with a design that he had drawn first on paper, or when he made wrought-iron lanterns and such things, Shad knew there wasn't a father quite like him in the world."--from **Copper-Toed Boots**. The gates still serve Mt. Hope Cemetery.*

The Tuttle Home in Lapeer.

in the wholesale grocery business and raised two children, Kathryn and Howard. When Shad moved his family east to Philadelphia in 1902, William and Maggie were the only Loffts left in Lapeer. Maggie's younger sister Sue, Mrs. Robert Jordan, was widowed in 1900 and she joined the Loffts in their home on St. Clair. Sue remained with them as a member of the household until William and Maggie died.

Sue was there, along with the other relatives, when the Loffts celebrated their fiftieth anniversary in September of 1912. Shad came from Philadelphia and Marguerite de Angeli mentions the celebration in her autobiography, as she and her husband Dai were able to attend, while en route to Canada..."A marquee was set up in the garden to accomodate the guests and serve refreshments. Among the gifts was a sugar and cream set of gold china, which I still have."

She also gives this vignette of her grandparents: "There at the table in her place was Grandma in her rocking chair telling Grandpa how to do each thing he had done for sixty years. Warm affection between them took the sting away from 'Now William...' "

William and Maggie made visits to see Shad and his family in the east during their later years, one of them in 1913, after Shad had moved to Collingswood, New Jersey. But the visits were not long ones, because the old blacksmith still kept his shop open in Lapeer. He worked until he was well past eighty, and then turned the business over to Tommy Oakes.

William Lofft was a great reader and it was a sorrow when his eyes failed him during his last years. But he continued to be healthy and cheerful, and as Marguerite remembered, "Grandpa Lofft gave one the feeling that the world was, on the whole, a happy place." He died very suddenly, at home in the old house on St. Clair, on February 14, 1924.

William Wise Lofft was past 86 when he died and the *County Press* called him "one of Lapeer's oldest and most highly respected citizens." The parlor of the house on St. Clair was filled with friends and relatives, including Shad and his wife from Collingswood, who came for the funeral. Reverend Karr selected a part of the 38th verse of II Samuel for his text: "Know ye not that there is a prince and a great man fallen this day in Israel?" William Lofft, Lapeer's longtime blacksmith, was buried in Mt. Hope Cemetery, where some of his handwork still served the entrance way in the form of the massive wrought iron gates.

Maggie Lofft lived on three years after her husband's death. Her sister Sue was a companion in the house when Maggie died in May 1927. She was called "one of Lapeer's pioneers" and praised as "one of the most ardent church workers through all her active years". As a "good neighbor" the *County Press* noted that she "leaves a large circle of friends and admirers." Maggie was the last of the Loffts in Lapeer, but the family's role as hardworking citizens of the town's early history lives on in Marguerite de Angeli's *Copper-Toed Boots*.

THE TUTTLES

Since 1872, a magnificent three-storied, many-gabled Queen Anne style mansion with porches and peaks and angles has attracted admiring glances where it has stood sentinel on the corner of North Main and State Streets in Lapeer. The house has been famous for its imposing qualities and beauty, and owners have carefully preserved its features. It has been home to only four owners in the century since it was built. The first owners of 610 North Main were the Tuttles, the family of Marguerite de Angeli's mother, Ruby.

Like his home, Columbus Tuttle occupied an important part of Lapeer. He was a lumber baron, a merchant, city official and the proprietor of a planing mill and door, sash and blind factory. He started out as a carpenter, learning that trade from his father, who brought the family from New York state to Macomb County, Michigan in 1836. Columbus married Eunice Hough in 1849 and the couple moved to Lapeer county in 1853. They lived in Almont before moving to Lapeer.

Columbus Tuttle became prosperous in the new community. He was in partnership with George Gregory and the men invested in town lots, opened a mercantile business along Nepessing and entered the retail lumber business. During the Civil War, Mr. Tuttle left his family and business to serve many months during 1864-1865 on a Federal gunboat along the Mississippi. Two years after the war's end, on September 28, 1867, Ruby Adele Tuttle was born to Columbus and Eunice, one of their six children. She was the mother of Marguerite de Angeli.

Ruby Tuttle and Shad Lofft met and courted through their school days in Lapeer. They were married when very young; Shad was 21 and Ruby was 19 on their wedding day, November 30, 1886. They had six children: Nina and Marguerite, born in 1887 and 1889 in Lapeer; Arthur, born in Chicago in 1894; Henry (Harry) and Walter, born in Lapeer in 1896 and 1901. The youngest, Richard, was born in 1905, after the family had settled in Philadelphia.

The Tuttle grandparents were not as well known to Marguerite and her siblings as Grandpa and Grandma Lofft. Eunice Tuttle died at 56, just a year before Marguerite's birth, and Columbus Tuttle died in 1895, when Marguerite was six. But their daughter Ruby Tuttle Lofft lived a long life, exerting much influence on her children, grandchildren and great-grandchildren. She was nearly 91 when she died in 1958.

Columbus Tuttle, pioneer lumber broker of Lapeer. He was the grandfather of Marguerite de Angeli.

Eunice Clement Tuttle, mother of Ruby, grandmother of Marguerite de Angeli

Lapeer's Second Ward School, Class of 1878, included Ruby Tuttle (Marguerite's mother) in the front row (wearing white), fourth from left. Other early Lapeer names in this picture include Tomlinson, Wadsworth, Powers, Keiser and Perkins.

Page 11

II. AN URGE TO WRITE AND DRAW

Marguerite de Angeli's birthplace on the corner of Main and Oregon. The one-lane dirt road is now M-24.

The birthplace house in 1986

So often I have tried to discover what it is that impels us to write or to draw. Perhaps it is because we want to record a happy moment, or try to convey our pleasure in something to others. Certainly it isn't because it is an easy way to make a living. It is the hardest kind of work. And like any project, there comes a point where only grim work will carry the thing to a conclusion. The excitement is long past, the end is not in sight, so one must just doggedly stick to it until it is done. That is true of writing a children's book or illustrating it. . . Yet some drive keeps me at it. —Marguerite de Angeli

At the corner of North Main Street and Oregon Road in Lapeer, Michigan stands a two-story frame house that was the birthplace of Marguerite Lofft on March 14, 1889. A century ago, the house stood at the edge of town and a narrow dirt street passed in front of it. Tall trees, remnants of the Michigan forest that had once covered the entire area, grew along the streets and in the grassy yards of the neighborhood. As Marguerite recalled, all Lapeer was "lovely and like a park."

Marguerite's earliest memories were all pleasant ones of warm family associations and happy living. Very early, she acquired a tendency to notice the minute spots of form and color in her surroundings and to glean images of the smallest details of life. An inborn urge to express herself creatively in words and pictures persisted through all her long life. This compulsion was soon recognized by her parents, Ruby and Shad Lofft and by her siblings, Nina, Arthur, Harry, Walter and Richard.

The leaning to creativity was a trait Marguerite inherited from earlier generations. Her Grandpa Lofft was adept at working in wrought iron; daily he curved iron into the mundane horseshoe as Lapeer's blacksmith, but he could also design and work grapes and leaves and vines from metal. Marguerite's father, Shad, was a photographer. He used shading and light and subtle posing of his subjects in his "gallery" on Nepessing Street and as a colorist, he did crayon enlargements of his photographs.

The multi-colors of her father's crayon box caught Marguerite's eye when she was two. In the moments of experimenting with the chalks, the joy of creating was born in her. It never left.

Along with the pleasing sensations of colors when applied to canvas or paper, fascination with the printed word came early to Marguerite. "My father," she recalled, "had large books over which I poured by the hour. They were too large for me to hold, but convenient to look at while lying on the floor. Some were bound copies of an Art Magazine, and in them were illustrations. . .painting and sculpture. . .architecture." From the age of three, Marguerite had a desire to create books of her own.

"Catholic Hill"

Memories of Lapeer as she grew up in the 1890s were happy. Relatives were plentiful and welcoming to the Lofft children; the woods were close to the boundaries of the little town and there were sights closely resembling pioneer days even when Marguerite was a child. Marguerite always remembered Christmas at Grandpa and Grandma Lofft's, sledding on Catholic Hill*, excursions to Lake Nepessing, and vignettes of "a cold winter day with snow on the ground. The sky was clear, and I walked down Main Street with my hand in my father's pocket."

And there were memories of many houses in Lapeer. The photography business was undependable in its cash returns, and Shad Lofft often moved his family from one rented house to another. Marguerite remembered moving nearly every year. Most of the houses still stand in Lapeer (see map of sites). They lived in the Wilson house, the Mahon house and the Cole house — those were all on Main Street. They lived in the Cox house near the new Catholic church and other assorted homes which were never far from Grandpa Lofft's or the Second Ward School where Marguerite and her sister attended. Most memorable for her was the Moore house on Calhoun Street.

"The Moore House" at 812 Calhoun.

Shad Lofft had taken a job in New York during a dry period for his Lapeer Studio, and while he was away the family lived in the commodious Moore house, with indoor plumbing and wide gardens outside. Marguerite was seven then.

It was during that era at the Moore house when Marguerite strongly sensed her creative impulse. "School in Michigan was delightful," she remembered, "because the more exacting phase of mathematics was still in the future, and Latin declension was to me unknown. As may be surmised, I didn't shine in those subjects. My romantic head was filled with pictures, with stories, and with visions of fame. . ." Often, her teacher at the Second Ward School would interrupt her thoughts, saying: "Marguerite, you're dreaming again. . ."

"Dreaming" to Marguerite was "wondering how I could put down in words the sheer joy in living which filled me to bursting, or how I could draw the moving shadows, the sunlight sifting through the leaves, the tree branches against the white house, or the stream of boys and girls themselves."

In April, 1902, when Marguerite was thirteen, a monumental change occurred. The Loffts left Lapeer, moving to Philadelphia where Shad was employed by the Eastman Kodak company as a demonstrator of the new film process which was replacing glass plate photography. The new home on 55th Street in West Philadelphia was a drastic departure in setting from the small-town atmosphere of Lapeer.

The Lofft children were soon "taking advantage of the wonders of a city, the museums, the parks, and the Public Library." Seeing the paintings and antiquities at Memorial Hall always intensified Marguerite's desire to draw, but about this time she pursued singing with a passion, worked with a private tutor, and as her mother said, "All she thought of was getting to be an opera singer."

This is a self-portrait in which Marguerite portrayed herself at 13, at the time of the move to Philadelphia. She included this picture in the book **Turkey for Christmas**.

As a high school student, Marguerite studied intensively with a voice instructor, Madame Suelke. Her concert contralto made her welcome in music circles where she sang arias
Marguerite told Dr. Jean Liming in an interview (1978) that "These cold days. . .I remember going to Catholic Hill in Lapeer. This is where a little, old Catholic church had been. . .back of that was quite a steep hill. This was two or three blocks from where we lived." The original Catholic Church stood on Calhoun Street, where Huron Street meets Calhoun. The topography of the area still suggests possibilities for sledding.

Page 13

and Lieder, and she was a regular member of several church choirs as paid vocalist. As a part of musical life of the area, she met John Dailey de Angeli, who played first violin with the Philadelphia Orchestra. He was an accomplished musician and the son of the theatrical agent who produced shows at the Steel Pier in Atlantic City. Dai (pronounced, Day) was also a "born salesman" his family recalls, who sold everything from Oriental rugs, Edison phonographs and sheet music at Grinnell's in Detroit.

Marguerite's singing talents reached professional status. Madame Suelke occasionally warned her that "You'll probably get married and have six children like your mother!" (Marguerite did). But the instructor was convinced that her pupil possessed much potential. She arranged an audition for Marguerite with Oscar Hammerstein I who was assembling an opera company for a world-wide tour. Marguerite was accepted as a cast member.

Her dilemma was great; should she attend the next Hammerstein rehearsal, or accept Dai's marriage proposal? She opted for life as Mrs. John de Angeli. In 1910, the couple was married in Toronto, where Dai was representing the Edison Company.

Marguerite's first years of married life were as mobile as her Lapeer childhood. She followed Dai all over western Canada where he was successful in establishing dealerships for the Edison phonograph sales. The de Angelis were in Minneapolis when their first child was born in 1911: John Shadrach, always called Jack. There were eventually five more: Arthur, Ruby Catherine (who died as an infant), Nina, Ted and Maury.

The de Angelis lived in Detroit in 1916, while Dai worked for J.L. Hudson Company. Marguerite found time to accept a position singing in an Episcopal church choir, and also attended her first art classes in downtown Detroit. She thrived in the atmosphere, but was soon called back to Collingswood, New Jersey to help nurse her dying sister Nina. Marguerite was at her parents' new home in Collingswood when Nina died on April 2, 1918.

Marguerite induced Dai to find work in the east, and the family settled near Marguerite's parents in Collingswood. There her busy family life, her occasional singing and performing, and Dai's participation in musical groups filled her life. But still she felt an itch to draw.

In the summer of 1921, when Marguerite was 32, she obtained the link she needed in developing her art. A neighbor-artist, Maurice Bower, was an illustrator for the Hearst publications. He agreed to tutor Marguerite, if she would give up her musical chores.

When Morry Bower judged Marguerite polished enough in her illustrating, he helped her obtain commissions for work. Her first published efforts appeared in Sunday school papers; quickly she branched out to include work for *St. Nicholas Magazine, The Ladies' Home Journal, The American Girl, The Country Gentleman* and regular jobs illustrating for writings of Elsie Singmaster, Cornelia Meigs, Dorothy Canfield and others. During that golden age of American magazine illustration, Marguerite de Angeli held a firm niche. For three consecutive years, her work appeared in print monthly.

Raising her five children and meeting publisher's deadlines was sometimes taxing. She found research necessary for some of her drawings, particularly those set in historical eras. There were trips to publishers' offices in New York and Philadelphia and long hours in her studio in the house in Collingswood where the de Angelis lived. But Marguerite was determined to combine homemaking with her career. "Sometimes I had a deadline to meet," she recalled, "and one of the boys would need a shirt, so I'd say, 'All right you iron it and I'll show you how.' I showed them how to do things and it came in very handy."

"I never shut them away from me," Marguerite said of those busy years of raising a family and pursuing a career. She ingeniously solved the problem of one-year old Ted's habit of climbing out of a playpen in her studio and on to the drawing table. "Finally, I put the playpen around me and the easel and let him have the run of the room. Everything was fine after that!"

Years elapsed, while Marguerite steadily illustrated for other authors, before she began

Marguerite in her thirties

her own career as a writer and artist. During the Depression, she was in New York hunting commissions and met an editor who suggested that Marguerite write a book for beginning readers and illustrate it herself. "I know you can do it," urged Helen Ferris of the Junior Literary Guild. "I know I can, too!" Marguerite exclaimed.

Dai de Angeli at age 8.

She returned home so excited that she immediately planned a dummy for the book she called *Ted and Nina Go To The Grocery Store.* It was published in 1936, starting her long and fruitful association with the Doubleday Company and with Peggy Lesser, her editor.

With Peggy Lesser as her enthusastic editor and Dai as a very supportive contributor to her research and editing and perfecting of story material and illustrations, Marguerite became a leading figure in the world of children's books. Her own lively curiosity kept story ideas coming and her exacting work kept her books outstanding.

In 1936, she published *Henner's Lydia,* about the Pennsylvania Dutch, doing on-site research in the Conestoga Valley. She traveled to the Gaspé Peninsula in Quebec for *Petite Suzanne* in 1937. *Copper-Toed Boots* in 1938 was her first venture into her own family background, followed by *Skippack School* in 1939. *Skippack School* dealt with the Mennonites and the humanistic teaching methods of schoolmaster Christopher Dock. *Thee, Hannah* was a Quaker story, with Philadelphia as a setting and Abolitionism as a sub-theme.

By 1940, Marguerite's sympathy in focusing on minorities and the foreign-born in America was well established. "Marguerite's caring nature for all humankind is reflected in her characters," notes Dr. Jean Liming of the Lapeer Community Schools. Her humanistic outreach in her stories was coupled with her consistent high degree of excellence in her work with words and pictures. That children are basically alike, no matter what their nationality or background, was a basic tenet of Marguerite's philosophy as a writer. "There are many differences in people," she said, "but each person has his place in the world."

In 1941, Marguerite published *Elin's Amerika,* a story based on early Swedish settlers in Delaware. *Up the Hill* (1942) was suggested by Polish friends who participated in Dai's music-making sessions. It was the story of a Polish-American family in a Pennsylvania mining town. In 1944, she recalled her Amish research experiences to produce *Yonie Wondernose,* which became a Caldecott Honor Book. Also that year, Marguerite wrote *Turkey for Christmas,* which resulted from her memory of the Loffts' first holiday after moving to Philadelphia.

For many years, Marguerite had wanted to write about a black child. "I wanted to see blacks included," she said, but her publishers shied away from a subject which might be considered "controversial". Finally, in 1946, Marguerite published *Bright April.* It broke literary ground; *Bright April* is considered to be the first modern children's book to discuss racial prejudice. With her accustomed sensitivity, Marguerite pointed out in *Bright April* that humans are basically one family.

*An illustration for **The American Girl.**
foretold the artist's excellence in portraying Middle Ages scenes, such as those which appeared in **The Door in the Wall.***

After years of living in the Philadelphia area, Marguerite and Dai settled in a converted summer cottage at Tom's River, New Jersey. The pleasant house, with an upstairs studio for Marguerite, was the scene of much productive work on books and illustrations, as well as the family life Marguerite and Dai always relished. Their children married, and Marguerite considered "that life is beginning again with the grandchildren." Jack married Edna, and had two children. Arthur and his wife Nina were parents of Kate. Nina and Alf Kuhn had three sons. Ted and his wife Betty had three children and Maury and Marianne added four sons to the de Angeli clan. Marguerite often used her thirteen grandchildren as models for book characters, just as she had her own children in the early part of her career.

Granddaughter Kate de Angeli Creitz vividly recalls the joy of watching Marguerite at work. "My most vivid memory of my grandmother is watching her sit on a stool painstakingly sketching, with a beautiful blue glass bowl of charcoal pencils and erasers and a bouquet of fresh flowers by her side," recalls Kate. "I'd exclaim: 'Oh, it's beautiful,' and she'd pause and examine it thoroughly and say, 'It'll do.' "

Marguerite de Angeli's double artistry, both in prose and in her illustrating, is perhaps one of the most monumental of its kind in books for children published during the twentieth century. The *Chicago Sun* said that "She fills each story with so many nice everyday details that all of the happiness which lies deep down in living seems to crop out." And Jacquie Piechowski, a Lapeer Art teacher, noticed the same qualities in the de Angeli illustrations: "She has a unique eye and a way of capturing life's everyday images and making them special. Her work is amazing. . .it has the qualities of Renoir, Degas and Mary Cassatt."

Marguerite when she won the Newbery Award.

Living in Tom's River suggested using the area as a setting, which Marguerite did in *Jared's Island,* published in 1947. But when she decided to select a British setting for what became *The Door in the Wall,* Marguerite was sent by her publisher to England. She and Dai explored the British Isles, which provided material for several forthcoming books.

In 1949 *The Door in the Wall* was Marguerite de Angeli's Newbery Award winner, an honor she was thrilled but incredulous to receive. Her increasing fame as a writer-illustrator was accepted with what Dr. Jean Liming calls "a becoming humility, suggesting that she has done only what any individual might." Following the awarding of the Newbery, Marguerite lived an increasingly "prized life," with countless recognitions of her talent and use of her skills in her books.

*Illustration from **Jared's Island,** published by Doubleday in 1947.*

In 1951, Marguerite's *Just Like David* was published. Following that, she launched a three-year spree of drawing which resulted in her *Book of Nursery and Mother Goose Rhymes.* The lavish illustrations gave new life to the old rhymes and perhaps gave Marguerite her affectionate title of "Everybody's Grandmother." The book was a Caldecott Honor title.

When Marguerite's book *Black Fox of Lorne* (a Newbery runner-up) appeared in 1956, she and her daughter Nina from Cincinnati had embarked on a trip to The Holy Land. Doubleday felt that first-person experience in the Middle East was essential for Marguerite's planned illustration for *The Old Testament.* She worked on those drawings for three years before the volume was published in 1960.

Marguerite showed no signs of retiring from her active career as writer-illustrator as she entered her seventies. When the family celebrated the de Angeli golden wedding in April, 1960, their setting was a cottage near Pennsburg, north of Philadelphia. Marguerite and Dai's sons were all living in that area and the cottage they bought was within a radius of several miles of children and grandchildren. During the winter months, Marguerite and Dai lived in Philadelphia.

Carolyn Field, President of the Philadelphia Booksellers Association, pays tribute to Marguerite de Angeli in February, 1966. To her left are Marguerite and Dai.

Marguerite's illustrations appeared in three books published during the early 1960's: *A Pocket Full of Posies, Book of Favorite Hymns* and *The Goose Girl.* With the books came honors. Marguerite was made a "Distinguished Daughter of Pennsylvania"; she received the Lewis Carroll Shelf Award for *The Door in the Wall.* She was honored by the Philadelphia Booksellers' Association, by Drexel Institute and by the Lit Brothers Good Neighbor Award. The Philadelphia Arts Council declared her among Philadelphia's "foremost authors in residence." She was cited by Governor Scranton in 1966 and the children's room of the Collingswood library was dedicated to her. In 1968, the Regina

Medal was awarded by the Catholic Library Association. At that time, Marguerite began her autobiography. She titled the book *Butter at the Old Price,* which she did not consider "dignified", but her son assured her it was not a "dignified" book!

Summing up her life and career was a major task, and showed Marguerite's continued versatility as a writer. In her own brand of hunt-and-peck typing, Marguerite recounted the many people, places and events which had contributed to her lifetime of creating story and picture. While the autobiography was being written, Dai died during the summer of 1969. Their sixty years together had produced a great family, but their partnership had also been a key to Marguerite's literary output. She often credited Dai's contributions, and dedicated her autobiography to her husband, "who always listened."

Marguerite and Dai

At eighty, Marguerite was still actively involved with family, friends and the world of books. She continued to appear as a speaker and frequently attended autograph sessions; she answered her voluminous mail and planned new books. *Fiddlestrings, The Lion in the Box* and *Whistle for the Crossing* appeared in the 1970s, when the author was in her eighties.

With each of her last books, Marguerite would declare that "I'm not going to do another." She accepted the fact that arthritis made her hands unsteady, but continued to turn out outstanding work. At 89, she told this writer that "I sent over some samples of a new way of sketching with ink and brush and they [Doubleday] were delighted with those." Constantly, new ideas for stories crept into her mind. Enthusiasm for her work continued unabated, and during the 1970's, Marguerite de Angeli was one of the few professional writers who could still live comfortably off book royalties alone.

*At the time of **Butter at the Old Price's** publication, 1971.*

Marguerite spent summers at her summer cottage, enjoying her children and grandchildren nearby, but returned to her apartment on Philadelphia's Parkway during the winter. She was a favorite resident in her building, and so enthused about her interesting neighbors that she started a book about them. Among her friends were Philadelphia's wealthiest dowagers, who called for her in limousines for performances of the symphony. She often invited family and friends for meals; she enjoyed cooking and tolerated no help in her kitchen.

Her optimistic nature was always her trademark, but certain aspects of modern life disturbed Marguerite. "Young people pass me and never thank me for holding the door," she noted. "But of course I blame the parents for a lot of it," she said. "I think children should be disciplined, not just allowed to go their own way. When born, they're innately good, but they haven't the experience and that has to be taught."

With her advancing age, it seemed that the tributes continued to become more frequent. In 1975, she was given the Bergman Award, which stated that "through her own life, she exemplifies the highest quality of man's humaneness to man." In 1976, she received an Honorary Doctorate from Lehigh University. In 1979, she was honored in Philadelphia and in Michigan on her ninetieth birthday and in 1982 Doubleday presented an achievement award in her name for professional development of librarians. When she was 95, Marguerite received the Girl Scouts' Juliette Low Award in 1984 and in 1985 she was inducted into the Michigan Women's Hall of Fame.

Her March 14th birthdays have been annually celebrated in both Philadelphia's Free Library and in the de Angeli Library in Lapeer. In both places, the events have brought hundreds of friends and admirers to congratulate her; there have been television cameras recording the events, performances of plays from her books and other tributes. B.A. Bergman mentioned in the *Philadelphia Bulletin* in 1980 that "I feel the birthday party should have been held in Veteran's Stadium. Even the stadium wouldn't hold all the peo-

Two Newbery authors: Lloyd Alexander greets Marguerite on her 91st birthday, March 14, 1980.

ple who would like to honor this fabulous woman who is 91 in years but not in spirit.''

'' Why is it I'm such a lucky woman?'' Marguerite has marvelled. But she claimed to know the reason why. As she said, ''Everything falls into place for me...Somebody's taking care of me, and I think He's taking care of all of us, but we have to be aware of it, to be open and aware. . .it's so wonderful the way I'm taken care of.''

In 1980, Marguerite de Angeli became a resident of Cathedral Village in Philadelphia. She immediately enjoyed the fellowship of other residents who lived in apartments or rooms in the complex, and as she said, ''I'm treated like a queen''. Residents all shared in the excitement of the publication of Marguerite's last book, *Friendship and Other Poems*, her many interviews, honors and her continuing output of sketches and drawings.

At the time of this writing, Marguerite de Angeli's ninety-eighth birthday approaches. She lives contentedly at Cathedral Village, magnificently serene, happy in her surroundings and appreciative of the people around her. ''I need people,'' she says. Nearly a century after her birth in Lapeer, Michigan, she still provides ''inspiration for a creative life to children and adults throughout the world.''*

Marguerite de Angeli at Drexel University with a group of librarians and authors. Left to right: Carolyn Field, Keith Doms, Marguerite, Nancy Larrick, Suzanne Hilton, Guy Garrison and Rosemary Webber.

The de Angeli family in 1948
Top: Ted, Maury, Dai, Jack and Arthur
Bottom: Betty, Nina, Marianne, Marguerite with Henry Kuhn, Edna with Tony, Nina Kuhn with Jeff, Nina de Angeli with David Kuhn.

III. COPPER-TOED BOOTS AND LAPEER

Shad and Ruby Lofft on their fiftieth wedding anniversary in November, 1936.

After publishing four books with Doubleday, Marguerite de Angeli turned to her own family background and the settings she remembered from her Lapeer girlhood for the book that forever identified her with Michigan and became one of the most enduring of her works. The story was *Copper-Toed Boots.* It is a tale of boyhood in Lapeer, as seen through the experiences of her father, Shad Lofft, and his childhood friend, Ash Tomlinson. The time period was the 1870s, but the people and places of Lapeer remained similar enough to those of Marguerite's own childhood that the book became a composite of her parents' memories, her own recollections and details and facts told by her relatives.

Marguerite had gained Peggy Lesser's enthusiastic response at Doubleday for a Michigan book, and she had broached the subject with her father, whom she planned to use as the hero of the story. But before she had progressed with the writing and illustrating, Shad Lofft died on January 17, 1937. The book project became a memorial to her father as well as a fifth volume to present to her publisher.

While the work for *Copper-Toed Boots* was underway in 1937, Marguerite was asked to speak about her writing career. "I am working on a story using Michigan as a background, based on incidents told me by my father of his childhood," she announced. "Altho I have lived for many years in Pennsylvania, I was born in Michigan and think of it as home. A child is scarcely conscious of why a certain place seems like home, but of late I have come to realize that the simple beauty of white houses with green blinds set back from a broad street lined with elms keeps calling me back..."

During the pre-writing of *Copper-Toed Boots,* Marguerite contacted Ash Tomlinson, both for permission to use his name and to question him about boyhood in Lapeer. Like Shad, Ash had left Lapeer and spent his adult life elsewhere. Ash lived in Cleveland when Marguerite first contacted him. Though he could well have stayed in Lapeer and succeeded his prosperous father in business, Ash Tomlinson was independent and struck out on his own while a teenager, first working as a bookkeeper in Duluth. Eventually, he owned Tomlinson Steamship Lines, a fleet which hauled iron ore from Duluth to Cleveland, and returned with coal.

Marguerite's initial contact with Mr. Tomlinson began with a letter...

My dear Mr. Tomlinson,

You won't know me, but I know you through my father who was your boyhood friend Shad Lofft of Lapeer.

Perhaps you already know that he died in January of this year.

I want to write and illustrate a child's picture book about early Lapeer and Papa's boyhood, using the little incidents that I've heard him tell. You are the other boy in the story and I would like to call you by your own name unless you object, because "Ash and Shad" are not commonly used and would add to the story.

I thought perhaps you would be willing to write and tell me some of the things you remember. Things you did as a young boy under ten or eleven, since the book will be for children of that age.

I had been talking to Papa about this for some time and now that he has passed on, I want to write it while it is fresh in my mind. I have heard about "Ash Tomlinson" ever since I can remember. He has told me about the "first & second woods", about finding the Indian skeleton out by hogback hill, about sleeping in your barn so as to get up early and see the circus come in, and about your going swimming in the Flint River at "Blue Clay"...

She traveled to Cleveland to visit Ash Tomlinson and then headed north to Lapeer to refresh her memory before finalizing her *Copper-Toed Boots* manuscript. Accustomed to the high-rises of Philadelphia and New York, she was surprised at the Lapeer she found in 1937. "The whole town seemed shrunken in size" she noted in her autobiography...buildings on Nipsing Street looked as if some giant weight had been dropped on them."

In her goal to attain historical accuracy and realism in describing Lapeer in the 1870s, Marguerite de Angeli painstakingly searched her own memory and those of her mother, Ash Tomlinson and other relatives who could supply details. Her pre-writing notes for the Lapeer book reveal her degree of depth in fact-gathering..."What did Ash call Mother & Father" queried one of her notes. And: "What did he call as he passed Shad's house on the way to school?" "What was Ash's mother's hired girl's name?"

Her own memory yielded many impressions and her notes reveal some antiquated vignettes of everyday living in Lapeer. To remedy Shad's "growing pains", His Pa "rubbed his legs with linament and his hands were rough and hard [from their long days in the blacksmith shop]. Goose grease--a tablespoon to take and then a piece of ham fat and red flannel tied around it and bottom of feet spread with magnetic ointment." So many details occurred to her that not all could fit into her story.

While spending a school day roaming in the Hogbacks, or trading treasures back and forth, or swimming in the Flint River were highlights for Shad and Ash in Copper-Toed Boots, nothing surpassed the excitement of the circus when it played Lapeer. That anticipation of the traveling troupes of circus animals and performers seized the entire town during Shad's boyhood. The *Clarion* noted the approaching spectacle in 1879, mentioning that

Lapeer folks are busting at the seams with excitement waiting for the arrival of The Great London Circus next week. 125 performers will be featured from Russia,

THE WOODS

A preliminary sketch for a decoration in **Copper-Toed Boots**.

A circus parade in Lapeer, facing west on Nepessing Street. Eight horses are seen drawing the steam calliope. Among the early circuses which came to Lapeer were the White Spear Show Company, Pawnee Bill's Wild West Show and Ringling Brothers.

Tomlinson home at Calhoun and Huron Streets

*Marguerite de Angeli at the time **Copper-Toed Boots** was published in 1938.*

Spain, France, Italy, and England. There will be 100 thoroughbred horses and 60 ponies, 10 monster elephants, 3 great bands, 20 golden chariots and an electric light with the illuminating power of 35,000 gas jets. It will all take place under a sea of tents with 168,000 yards of canvas.

One of the "monster elephants" stole the show during the circus described in *Copper-Toed Boots* in a performance that became a legend in Lapeer for decades to follow. During the course of the circus parade down Nepessing Street, a recalcitrant elephant broke loose, storming across the courthouse lawn and onto Court Street. The effect was enormous, and Marguerite captured the excited melee in both a color page of illustration and her own prose in *Copper-Toed Boots*.

Because the elephant story was so entrenched in Lapeer's past, old-timers were hard to reconcile when *Copper-Toed Boots* appeared, placing the incident in the early 1870s. Actually, the elephant runaway happened when Shad Lofft was 17, in the early 1880s.

Despite the shifts in time sequences, *Copper-Toed Boots* was essentially a true collection of factual anecdotes, transformed into Marguerite de Angeli's skilled story-telling style. The book abounds in characters who actually peopled the town in the 1870s and 1880s.* The Tomlinson family was prominent in the community during the era described in *Copper-Toed Boots* and despite the fact that they were wealthy and the Loffts were middle-class, Shad and Ash were inseparable. The proximity of their homes made the friendship convenient. Samuel Tomlinson, Ash's father, was a merchant, a coach, wagon and sleigh maker as well as the publisher of the *Lapeer Clarion*. His substantial home was located at the corner of Calhoun and Huron Streets, kitty corner from the first Catholic church and rectory. The Lofft home was just two blocks west. It was at the Tomlinson home where the boys waited for the circus train all night. In the late 1870s, Mr. Tomlinson moved his family to a more pretentious house on Pine Street and Shad undoubtedly was a frequent visitor there. Years later, in 1924, the Pine Street House became Lapeer's hospital.

When *Copper-Toed Boots* was published by Doubleday in October, 1938 it made a great impact on Lapeer and was quickly adopted as a standard text in many Michigan elementary schools. Marguerite was delighted at the response her Michigan book received, and she was especially pleased when Ash Tomlinson responded to the book with great pleasure. He invited Marguerite, Dai and Ruby Lofft to take a Great Lakes cruise on one of his ore ships from Buffalo to Duluth. "A delightful end to the *Copper-Toed Boots* experience," Marguerite remarked.

The career of *Copper-Toed Boots* has been a never-ending one. It has gone through dozens of printings, including an edition in England. Generation after generation of Michigan school children read or listen to teachers read the story of Shad and Ash and old Lapeer. As one child observed, "They had so much fun back then!"

Many graphic passages of description of everyday existence and social mores of Lapeer in the 1870s were excised from the *Copper-Toed Boots* manuscript to provide for a streamlined plot progression to interest young readers.*

Two pivotal episodes in *Copper-Toed Boots* which involved Shad Lofft were also firm-

The mention of Joe Knight as school janitor in Copper-Toed Boots struck a responsive chord with many former Lapeer students. Joe was born of slave parents in Alabama, but brought north by a soldier returning from the Civil War. For fifty years he served as school janitor and was much beloved by his community.

ly entrenched incidents of Lapeer lore: the prank of tying the calf in the schoolhouse belfry and the famous elephant runaway during the circus parade in Lapeer. Mrs. de Angeli admitted to this writer that while the stories were true, she used "poetic license" in the time of each event. She stressed, however, that "the other things in the story were nearly all factual, including the calf in the belfry."

It appears that the calf prank was the product of Shad and Ash as high school students, rather than as the little boys described in *Copper-Toed Boots*. The school building with the belfry, where Shad and Ash tied the calf's tail to the bellrope was the old Lapeer Academy, which was used by the local school system until 1965. The imposing building was built by the White family in their "Whitesville" end of Lapeer, in hopes that the county would select the building as court house. When the Whites' building was rejected in favor of the Hart structure, which was closer to the business district, the losing contender became the town's high school. The present Administration Building of the Lapeer Community Schools stands on the spot.

According to the *Lapeer Clarion*, pranks like Shad's and Ash's were commonplace annoyances in town, and such offenses and offenders were roundly scolded by the newspaper. On May 31, 1879, the paper mentioned that "Any young man who has no more sense than to hitch a horse to a shade tree should be made to pay for his ignorance and the tree besides. This is the view Justice Barber took. He fined the young ignoramus $10."

The school in Shad Lofft's time

Shad Lofft in 1886 (age 21)

RESIDENCE OF S. J. TOMLINSON

The second Tomlinson house on Pine Street

Old Lapeer High School, where the calf was tied in the belfry. This photo was taken the day the building was slated for demolishment in 1965. The present Lapeer Community Schools Administration Building now occupies the site.

See Appendix I in this book for several unpublished anecdotes from the original Copper-Toed Boots manuscript.

IV. LAPEER SHARES THE LIMELIGHT

Following the publication of *Copper-Toed Boots*, Marguerite de Angeli continued to return to Lapeer regularly. As a foremost creator of children's literature, she was often summoned to speak, to autograph and appear as an author, but she preferred the informal visits in Lapeer, where she mingled informally with the people she felt appreciated her the most.

In 1941, Marguerite was asked to appear at the University of Michigan. Although public speaking was a trial for her, she always managed to entertain audiences with her warm, earthy speaking style, her humor and her firm insight into the child's world. But prior to any formal appearance, Marguerite struggled with fearful anticipation.

It was always her husband Dai who managed to assure her. When she was feeling nervous pangs at an invitation as formidable as the one from the University of Michigan, Dai would urge her to "let the tears flow!" "Turn on the spigot and get it over," he would tease. He prodded Marguerite and joked with her and successfully brought each speaking engagement into manageable perspectives. "Just get up, say it, and sit down!" he advised.

Her 1941 Michigan trip included a Lapeer visit, and another formal invitation to Flint. To open Book Week in November, the Flint Institute of Arts and the Friends of the Library sponsored her. Marguerite was greeted by 200 of her admirers at Flint's art institute, where she discussed her books, drew charcoal sketches of some of her characters, and signed copies of her works. *The Flint Journal* noted that "It's no wonder that children and grownups too find Marguerite de Angeli's books charming. . .her local admirers discovered that the author and illustrator is equally as charming in person."

In 1950, while Marguerite was en route to the crowning achievement of her career, the awarding of the Newbery, she included a visit to Lapeer. The medal was awarded at the American Library Association's July, 1950 meeting in Cleveland, but Lapeer shared the pre-award excitement when Marguerite arrived at the library's informal reception for her on the afternoon of July 16.

*Marguerite's visit to Lapeer in 1950 was en route to the awarding of her Newbery Medal. At the library, copies of **Copper-Toed Boots** were signed for Donald Muir (right) and standing, left to right: Marshall Smith, Tom Bogardus, Wayne Smith, Arthur Bush and Robert Ferner.*

Margaret Caffall and her staff greeted the many Lapeer friends who came to congratulate Marguerite on the library lawn. As usual, the guest of honor autographed piles of her books, met many of her young readers, and greeted old friends. Linking her Lapeer girlhood with her present position as a celebrated author was Marguerite's old Sunday School teacher from the Baptist church, Anna Webster Laing. Old timers at the reception discussed again the incidents in *Copper-Toed Boots*. Congressman Louis Cramton and Marguerite's cousin

Harold Tuttle guessed they were the only ones present who had known Grandpa Lofft. Mr. Cramton remarked that he still prized a desk made by Mr. Lofft, and that many people had begged to buy the fine piece of cabinetry built by Lapeer's pioneer blacksmith.

"I always take every opportunity I can to come here," Marguerite said. "It's always such a thrill to come back." And she continued to return to her roots in Lapeer. Soon after Drexel Institute of Technology honored her in November, 1963 with a special citation "for her distinguished and lasting contribution to the World of Children's Books", Marguerite and Dai came to Lapeer to visit relatives. As usual, *The Lapeer County Press* reported on her current activities. "I feel exactly the same inside as I did when I lived here," she assured the *Press*. And the interviewer remarked that "Marguerite de Angeli, 74, has long belonged to Philadelphia. But her heart, which never grew old, belongs to Lapeer. Many Lapeer children know Mrs. de Angeli. So do children in Holland, England and Albania. She speaks in their language through her rare ability to open doors in young hearts and minds."

Dai's failing health prevented him from traveling in his last years (he died in 1969), but Marguerite still accepted calls to appear at universities and book festivals. Though her honors had continued to accumulate, she was thrilled when the important Regina Medal of the Catholic Library Association was awarded her in 1968. This medal noted Marguerite's "Continued Distinguished Contribution to Children's Literature" when it was awarded in St. Paul.

Once again, the glory was shared with Lapeer. On her way back to Philadelphia, Marguerite stopped off in Lapeer. She was again welcomed to the Lapeer library, where she brought the silver medal she had been awarded. Marguerite was deeply pleased with the inscription which appeared on her heavy, silver medal: a quote from Walter de la Mare, which summed up her own work:

Only the rarest
Kind of best in Anything can
Be good enough for the
Young.

During her post-Regina Award visit, the *County Press* again interviewed Marguerite, finding her "dressed in bluebird blue, as full of warmth and charm as a spring day." She was full of plans, too. She announced that she was writing her autobiography, and the visit included some refreshing of her memory of life in Lapeer. One of her goals was achieved, as she found most of the girlhood homes around town she had lived in before the peripatetic Loffts finally moved to Philadelphia.

A number of Lapeer people, realizing the importance of the town's famous native, were determined to honor her themselves. In May of 1971, coinciding with the publication of Marguerite's autobiography, *Butter at the Old Price*, a whole week of festivities was planned. It resulted in what Marguerite called "the week of my life."

Lapeer friends, educators, librarians and admirers created a succession of exciting tributes to Marguerite during her homecoming. The Lapeer County Historical Society, the Lapeer County Library and the Lapeer Public Library organized book signings, school visits, a banquet and the unveiling of an historic marker at her birthplace.

The highlight — and there were many highlights during the week-long visit to Lapeer — came on May 20, when "Our Evening with Marguerite de Angeli" was celebrated in the Methodist church building of the same congregation in which her well-loved Lofft

BIRTHPLACE
OF
MARGUERITE
LOFFT deANGELI
Author and Illustrator

LAPEER COUNTY
HISTORICAL SOCIETY

Mrs. de Angeli, age 82, greets friends at Trinity Methodist Church in Lapeer.

Autographing at the Lapeer Library

Marguerite visits with the Jessop family and Peter Chellberg (left) on June 4, 1978 at a reception at Zemmer Junior High in Lapeer.

grandparents were so actively a part many years before. 250 of her Lapeer friends crowded in, only half of those who tried for tickets to the event. Marguerite arrived at the church on the sunny spring evening in true pioneer fashion — by horse and buggy. "Mrs. de Angeli's smile never faltered," remarked the *County Press.* "At 82, she looked as charming as any young deb in her long-sleeved white blouse and black velvet skirt."

"The Great Americans", a singing group, serenaded Marguerite with an original song titled appropriately, "Copper-Toed Boots", written by Ron Jarvis and Lapeer teacher Ken Nelson. Mayor Connor welcomed her in the name of the city, saying, "In reading your book I can see your love and admiration for this community and I'm sure you can see it is reciprocated."

James Jessop of the Lapeer Schools summoned diners at the banquet with the sound of the old school bell which had been saved from the former high school — the same school bell which sounded with Shad's and Ash's prank — and it rang for the first time in six years.

At the head table with Marguerite were her son Arthur and his wife Nina, her sister-in-law Alma, and cousins she had not seen in sixty years, Mr. and Mrs. Fred Lofft from St. Mary's, Ontario.

Gifts and presentations were given to Marguerite, and the sign was unveiled which would soon mark her birthplace. The most unexpected presentation was a photo of herself as a baby, taken by her father, on a "bear rug".

Marguerite, in her response, regaled her Lapeer audience with highlights from her writing career, noting that many events came almost magically to her as "miraculous experiences." But the usually prolific user of words had to admit she had no words to describe how she felt during this most memorable of her visits back to Lapeer.

"I hope my father and mother know about it all. . .I like to think so," Marguerite remarked as she considered all the exciting events during her Lapeer homecomng week. "I shall keep the memory forever."

During her triumphant week back home, Marguerite was often asked what her next writing project would be. She had considered *Butter at the Old Price* her last book, but while adjusting to the loss of her husband Dai, she wrote and illustrated a book about his boyhood, *Fiddlestrings,* which was published in 1974. She described herself then as "an old lady in my eighties. I am homely and have white hair, which I like more than the mousy brown color it was before. I have blue eyes, still good to see with, and I talk and walk very straight for one my age. I am happy here in Philadelphia and very fortunate to have many friends. I also have a little house in the country among my four sons's families where I go in the summer. Besides, twice a year or so I visit my daughter and her family in Cincinnati. I miss my dear husband, but we were married for almost sixty years before he died."

"My life is full. At this point I just want to put things in order and leave this life with grace. I have started a story about my friends who live in my apartment house, which is an unusually friendly place. This may never become a book, but it gives me an objective to work toward."

Her dedication to her work, and persistent urge to write and illustrate, produced another two titles, *The Lion in the Box* (1975) and *Whistle for the Crossing* (1977). For the latter, a series of trips to the Franklin Institute supplied the research she needed for the railroad story she set in the 1850s. Attendants hoisted Marguerite up into the engines for first hand looks at the antique locomotives.

"I always thought I was the homeliest girl in Michigan", Marguerite said, but when she used the same adjective to describe herself in her eighties, those who knew her disagreed. Instead, she perfectly fit her unofficial title of "Everybody's Grandmother". She had remained tall and straight, had snow-white hair rolled into a bun and sparkling blue eyes behind silver-rimmed glasses. Always appearing cheerful and enthusiastic, her usual method of greeting old Lapeer friends and young admirers was with a sincere hug and kiss.

Lapeer grew to expect her springtime visits. She made additional friends each year, through her visits to schools, libraries and in various homes around town. But very few relatives remained during the 1970's. Marguerite's usual hostess was her cousin, retired teacher Ruth Turnbull.

With Peter Chellberg (1978)

"She felt her roots were here and she was at home when she came to Lapeer," remarked Ruth Turnbull. One of her rituals was a ride around town, past the houses she knew and the sites of childhood. On one drive, Marguerite stopped at the Wilson house on Main Street where she had lived, and toured the old home. Another time, the Riddells, who lived in her Grandfather Tuttle's magnificent Main Street house, ushered her up to the attic where she had played as a girl. That same attic served as setting for *Ted and Nina Have A Happy Rainy Day.* And seeing the Michigan countryside in springtime always thrilled Marguerite! On one drive, the muse struck her and she penned a poem for her cousin, focusing on the natural beauty she saw.

Marguerite was 89 and in fine form when she made her May, 1978 return. Dr. Jean Liming, librarian for the Lapeer schools, had visited Marguerite in Philadelphia, taping interviews and photographing slides of the author at home. Dr. Liming arranged a Sunday afternoon open house at Zemmer Junior High and while Marguerite watched the slides she quipped, "Who's the old lady?" As usual, she autographed piles of books, and spoke to the crowd, expressing her love for Lapeer and sharing her present and future plans. As usual, a group of awe-struck children gathered around her. Mark Jessop, then eight, told his parents he didn't intend to wash his hand, since it had touched the hand of a famous writer!

With Beth and Mark Jessop

"I am in constant wonder at the marvels of the world," Marguerite noted. "The growing things, such as tiny flowers hiding in the woods, the immensity of mountains, trees. And oh, the wonders of the human body — of hearing and sight. I think it is my eternal optimism that has kept me young. It is also love. . ."

And that love of Lapeer was always evident when Marguerite de Angeli came home.

V. THE NINETIETH BIRTHDAY YEAR

Awareness that Marguerite de Angeli's ninetieth birthday was approaching on March 14, 1979 led an eighth grade English class at White Junior High to ask Governor William Milliken to recognize Lapeer's author. The goal was the declaration of March 14 as Marguerite de Angeli Day throughout the state. Students researched and presented significant reasons why Lapeer's famous author should be honored by an executive proclamation; they drafted their proposal as a classroom project, sending it on to Lansing.

Many weeks later, the students were enthused when a letter from Governor Milliken arrived, praising them for "thoughtfulness and creativity in wishing to honor the life and works of ...Marguerite de Angeli." He added that "You might be interested in knowing that I have a general policy against naming days for living persons. However, I felt that your gesture was inspiring enough to warrant a rare exception." With the Governor's letter was the official proclamation declaring "Marguerite de Angeli Day in Michigan" on March 14.

The official proclamation and student letters were forwarded to Marguerite in Philadelphia, and she responded by describing her excitement at the honor given her by her home-state...

"How can I thank you for all your effort...? About 9:30 the other night I had just come in from an evening with friends when our security man of this apartment brought me a large official looking package. What could it be? I took it to the kitchen counter so there would be room to open it. Can you inmagine my surprise and delight when I found your birthday card with its copper-toed boot and the Proclamation...due to your efforts? It was almost more than I could take in. I still can't quite realize that March 14 is to be Marguerite de Angeli Day throughout Michigan! .. I have read all your names and send my LOVE to you all. Perhaps I shall see you in the spring..."

Although Marguerite was committed to attend the annual birthday party held for her at the Free Library of Philadelphia, Lapeer's City Branch Library went ahead with a party in her honor. Lapeer school children brought donations and dozens of roses were sent to the author, along with hundreds of letters and drawings. If she had been able to be more than one place on her ninetieth, Marguerite would have joined 350 guest at the Lapeer library party.

March 14, 1979 in Philadelphia was an "overwhelming" day for Marguerite. Citations from Mayor Rizzo and the Governor of Pennsylvania were delivered to her home along the Parkway, along with stacks of birthday mail, gifts and deliveries of flowers. Hundreds of her friends and family members attended the party held at the Free Library of Philadelphia, where Carolyn Field read Rachel De Angelo's special poem:

Oh to be in Philly now that spring is here
to celebrate a birthday of one we hold most dear.

A very special birthday, surpassing all the rest
For Marguerite is 90 and still the very best...

What did she plan to do during her next decade? she was asked. "I'm going to have a lot of fun!" was Marguerite's response.

Part of that fun included a trip to Lapeer in May. Her granddaughter Kate de Angeli Creitz was living in Dearborn and Marguerite was anxious to see her great-grandson, Colin. She also had on her list of activities a visit to White Junior High in Lapeer, to meet the students who had been responsible for the official celebration of her birthday that spring.

When she arrived in the classroom with her cousin, Marguerite typified her "Everybody's Grandmother" status. To a classroom hushed with excitement and awe, she sat down to visit, and tell stories about her own school days in Lapeer. She patiently answered the students' questions and seemed reluctant to leave when the period was over. As she left she remarked, "It is hard for me to realize that all this honor has come to me and--I love you all!"

Courtesy of the Free Library of Philadelphia.

Surrounded by members of her family in the Skyline Room of the Free Library of Philadelphia on March 14, 1979, Marguerite receives an oversized greeting depicting highlights from her books.

Marguerite de Angeli's memorable visit to the Lapeer classroom was filled with interesting reminiscences of her life and career. The following excerpts are highlights of her conversation with the students, their teacher Bill Anderson, and the author's cousin Ruth Turnbull.

DE ANGELI: *"I love seeing you all and I thank you for all your wonderful flowers and letters, drawings and everything... I appreciate every single one. It took me a long time to read them all and I have a pile of big envelopes 'that high' of drawings and letters from Lapeer. I didn't know HOW I was going to answer them and then a friend of mine said, 'Now for a birthday and friendship gift, I'll do this typing for you.' So, I wrote a letter that I hoped would say everything...you have the letter, I expect... and she made eighteen copies; she didn't Xerox any of them or use carbon paper, but made separate ones and sent the envelopes and got them all ready and did that for me. We spent four hours going through those envelopes!"*

ANDERSON: *"We all went over and cut the first piece of birthday cake at your party at the library."*

DE ANGELI: *"The Main Library in Philadelphia had a birthday party for me and there were about 200 people there; they had a cake. Last year, they had a party for me too and had a cake in tiers, but I didn't see it until it was pretty well done, but I had a piece of it. My family was there and some of my friends from the building where I live. My doctor was there and my grandson who happened to be home over the weekend. He's in the Air Force learning to fly the big jets."*

TURNBULL: *"You might like to know that she read every letter that came and every name..."*

DE ANGELI: *"...Until I came to one ten feet long from the library!"*

ANDERSON: *"Our names were on that, too."*

DE ANGELI: *"But I tell you, I've got all the letters on the floor in my study and I love them all."*

TRACY: *"Mrs. de Angeli, what was Lapeer like when you were living here as a child?"*

DE ANGELI: *"Oh! It was a small town; it's grown a great deal. I think there were about--would you say, 2500 people here?"*

TURNBULL: *"I doubt there were that many."*

ANDERSON: *"We all know where your birthplace is, of course."*

DE ANGELI: *"You do! There's a sign there, isn't there?"*

ANDERSON: *"Andrea, you've been in Marguerite's grandparents' home haven't you?"*

ANDREA: *"Well, it's green now and has a fence around it and it still has a porch on the side...there hasn't been that much remodeling."*

DE ANGELI: *"You know, I made that picture on the end-papers [of **Copper-Toed Boots**] from memory and when my mother saw it, she said, 'How did you ever remember that's the way it looked?'"*

ANDREA: *"We used to live on the same block."*

ANDERSON: *"Mrs. de Angeli, can you tell us how you first heard the expression 'butter at the old price' and how you decided to call your autobiography that?"*

DE ANGELI: *"Well, you know, as I remember Nipsing Street, not Main Street, Nipsing Street...you know where the Court House is, all of you, well, across the side street was Uncle Denny's jewelry store, and that's Miss Turnbull's grandfather. And I used to love to go in there and he was very kind to me...so then across from that, on Nipsing Street, was my father's photograph gallery--on the second floor." [Above the former Zemmer Drug Store.] "...Anyway, two or three doors down was my Uncle Charley's grocery store. Then down further, across the street was Uncle Steve Lockwood's general store. And do you know, do you remember, maybe it isn't true anymore, but it used to be that a general store had in the front dry goods, yard goods. Of course we didn't have store clothing at that time. Everybody made their own, or had a seamstress. Then, the next section would be, china, kitchen-ware. Then, after that would be the grocery department. When women used to come in on Saturday and bring their butter to sell in exchange for other commodities and my Aunt Ella, who lived way down--oh, about a mile out of town, used to make very good butter. She was meticulous about the way she made it. So she always had top price for her butter. Well, there was a Mrs. Desireau, who lived out Davison Road, who was somewhat less a perfect housekeeper and when she made her butter and brought it in, my uncle didn't sell it, because he said you could find 'most anything in her butter. So, she complained one time that she didn't get top price for her butter like Mrs. Tuttle did. Well, Uncle Steve said, 'If you're as careful as Mrs. Tuttle is about making your butter, I'll be glad to give you top price.' So she went home determined that next time she would get top price for her butter…Well, it was a hot day, and in those days, you had to have a cookstove going, because people ate dinner in the middle of the day. So, while Mrs. Desireau was working the water out of the butter, she had to get up to mend the fire. So she put the butter bowl down on the floor, under the table. And there were two or three little tads running around without very much on because it was hot and one of them slipped and sat down in the butter! So, she slatted the butter off him back into the bowl and said 'butter'll have to go at the old price again!' ''*

"Now this is a story my Uncle Steve told so how true it is, I don't know! But then-- that became a family saying, you see, and whenever things didn't go as we hoped they would, we would say, 'Oh no, butter'll have to go at the old price again!' ''

"Have any of you read **The Door in the Wall?** *Do you know that book? Well, I thought I'd been so careful in drawing it that I was hoping the title page would look something like a monk's manuscript. Well, of course it didn't! I was so disappointed that I didn't look at the book again for about a week and then I said, 'butter'll have to go at the old price again!' ''*

"Do you want to tell me a story?''

Telling of early life in Lapeer at White Junior High. Her cousin looks on.

JOHN: *"What was your first book that you started writing?''*

DE ANGELI: *"Ted and Nina Go to the Grocery Store; it was for little first graders to read to themselves.''*

SKIP: *"How'd you get involved in writing?''*

DE ANGELI: *" You see, ever since I can remember, when I was about three years old I think, I wanted to write and illustrate books. Ever since I knew what books were. But it was always very difficult to get out of my mind the picture I saw there-on to the paper. Maybe you all know about that. Do you? It's one thing to see it in your mind and another thing to get it down on paper. Well, when I was about six-teen, I was singing one afternoon with my sister's accompaniment, just making believe I was an opera singer, never thinking about anybody else. We were having a good time and the minister who lived across the street came over and he said, 'No, I don't want to see your mother, especially, I want to see you. How would you like to be the contralto in our quartette which we are just forming?' Oh! of course I would like to; of course I would! Now he said you must take lessons, to be a professional. Then it happened that my father, my mother and I found a teacher, the best teacher in Philadephia--because she taught the easy way of singing. She would say to me, 'Now Marguerite, drop your arms; don't raise your shoulders, now sniff your breath; now SING!' And you could sing, sing, sing on that method, because everything was relaxed. Now you remember that if any of you want to be singers. So, it happened then, that I sang that first year in church for quite a long time and then someone of-fered me another position and I kept on singing professionally and then, I met my husband and I had the opportunity to sing with Oscar Hammerstein. Not the one you would have heard about, perhaps, but his uncle or his father. In our Philadelphia opera house. And he took me, with his Metropolitan opera company. So I was going to be an opera singer. So I couldn't fit all that in with drawing, see…Then, after the rehearsal, my parents sat with me and said 'have you realized how difficult it would be, how much you would be away from home, and away from Dai'-who was then my fiance--I was engaged to him. No, I hadn't thought of that. 'Have you realized how difficult it would be to rear a family--if you're an opera singer?' No, I hadn't thought about that. 'Don't you think you'd be happier not following an opera career?' Yes, I think I would--and I never went to another rehearsal!'' ''And I have a lovely family. I listened to my parents! I had six children; we lost one baby. I have five wonderful children and I have thirteen grandchildren and five great-grandchildren.''*

RUSSELL: ''What was your first book to win a Newbery Award?''

*DE ANGELI: ''**Door in the Wall**--and you want to know how that came about?'' ''Well, my husband was a violinist and he played first violin under the first two conductors of the Philadelphia Orchestra. Do you know that the Philadelphia Orchestra is a very special one? It's known all over the world. At that time you could not make a living out of playing with the orchestra. It meant that you had to do other things-- play in the evenings and things of that sort. So he decided to do something else. But we always had quartettes. It happened that someone among our friends invited us along with three or four other people to join and that became a regular thing. Every two or three weeks we met and many times it was at our house. Among those who played was Harmon Robinson who had had a very serious illness when he was about ten, so that he was in bed for three years. And when he got out of bed he could walk only with his hands on his knees to support his torso, or with crutches. He was all right sitting, but when he stood, he was bent over. But he was such a charming person, everybody loved him, everybody wanted to be near him and talk to him and what I mean to say is--he was a successful person. You see what I mean? And I thought 'wouldn't it be nice to write a book about a boy who is handicapped--and yet can be a successful person?' I was so taken with the idea that I found it hard to finish the drawings for **Jared's Island** do you know that book? Well, that's another story. But I finished it and then I began on **The Door in the Wall** and went to England to get material and I read about medieval--because I always wanted to do a story about that period, because of the costumes.''*

ANDERSON: '' Marguerite, how was it that your family left Lapeer? Why did they go to Philadelphia?''

DE ANGELI: ''Oh, my father was with the Eastman Kodak company and they sent him to Pennsylvania to all-new territory, so we moved to Philadelphia when I was fourteen. I guess all you boys and girls are older than that. How old are you dear?''

ANDREA: ''Thirteen''

DE ANGELI: ''I hope when you get to be ninety, you don't forget, like I'm doing!''

DEBBIE: ''Of all your books, which is your favorite one?''

*DE ANGELI: ''That would be very hard to tell, because there's an association with each one that makes that very special. All these things that happened...such as the lock of hair. Do any of you know **Black Fox of Lorne?** Well, that book came out of a visit to Scotland. We went to Skye and I had no idea of getting material for a book because I had been doing the nursery rhymes and I was quite tired. It took me three and a half years to do that. So I went there for a rest and vacation. Well, we went to watch them bring in fish on the west coast of Scotland, before we went to Skye. And I saw two little boys about so high and they were identical twins, laughing and punching each other as boys do and 'Oh I have an idea!' and my husband said,*

'Well what is it?' and I said 'Oh I can't tell you, it's too fragile and I have to keep it a secret.' Before you begin, if you tell too much, it goes away; you've lost your interest. Later that day, my husband went to get his hair cut and I went with him in this little village and a woman cut his hair, so we were talking and I told her about seeing these little boys. She said, 'They're my sister's children. They're always taking each other's place and fooling people because they are so much alike.' 'Oh! There's another idea, you see! I wanted to set the story back in about the ninth century, because there were so many place names sounding Scandinavian and I knew that at that time the Vikings invaded Scotland. And I found out later that some of my ancestors were fighting in that period.''

ANDREA: *''What other places did you go to get research for your books?''*

DE ANGELI: *''Well, Scotland and England mostly, but I went up into the Pennsylvania Dutch country for* **Henner's Lydia** *and* **Yonie Wondernose** *and* **Skippack School,** *to study the Mennonites and the Amish people.''*

TURNBULL: *''You went to the Holy Land, too, Marguerite.''*

DE ANGELI: *''Oh yes, of course...I suggested to my editor that I do selections from the Old Testament and illustrate them and the Doubleday Company sent me to the Middle East and I took my daughter with me and we were gone three weeks, so that I could get the feeling. Unless you've been there, you can't realize how little shadow there is. There's so much reflected light and that has to be taken into consideration with the pictures, you see. When we went to Greece, there was still some of that reflected light.''*

JOHN: *''What was the last book you've done?''*

DE ANGELI: *''***Whistle for the Crossing***--do you know that one, at all? It's about a boy whose father drove the first engine from Philadelphia to Pittsburg, all on the Pennsylvania line. And that's a true story. I mean to say the essence of it is true. A friend came to see me with his wife and brought a little engine that he made out of plumbing supplies, hoping I'd be interested--and I was.''*

TURNBULL: *''She had to go up and crawl up in the cab of the engine.''*

DE ANGELI: *''Oh, yes! I went to the museum in Philadelphia and there was an enormous engine, much larger than the dimensions of this room, but on the other side, there are two smaller engines of that period I spoke of, about 1852. So I had been in there, but I couldn't get up into this engine myself, so I asked for somebody to send a man with me and boost me up into the engine so I could see how everything worked. How you blow the whistle and how you ring the bell for the crossing and I saw where the engineer could rest once in a while in a seat that turned down and I used to think that a steam engine--that that long boiler was filled with water--even up 'til then, mind you, and that's only two years ago. But it's not filled with water; it's filled with pipes filled with water and that's quite different. I learned those things about the engine before I wrote the story.''*

ANDERSON: *''Did you have some interesting experiences when you went into the Pennsylvania Dutch country to research the Amish people?''*

DE ANGELI: *''YES!'' ''It took me all of one day...you see, when I thought about this, and I can't remember how this idea came to me...I talked about it a good deal,* because I didn't know where to go to get material. I read a book, first of all, about the making of Pennsylvania and learned about the Amish and the Mennonites, who are separate religious sects. The Mennonites wear very plain clothes; the dresses may have a little pattern in them but the Amish may not have any pattern in them. Now, they're changing; they're not nearly as rigid as they were, but this was a good many years ago; I think it was about 1935.''

SKIP: "Have you ever thought about moving back to Lapeer?"

DE ANGELI: "No, because I have lots of friends in Philadelphia and--where would I live? I guess I could live with Ruth!"

TURNBULL: "She's needed to be close to her publisher."

DE ANGELI: "And I have four sons who live within a three-mile radius of each other and they're all friends, isn't that great? And I love my daughters-in-law, so I want to be near them."

TRACY: "Do you have any books you are planning to write now?"

DE ANGELI: "No, I don't plan to do any more. I have written some poetry that I sent to the publisher and I think that they will publish it. Over a period of years, I've written this and I'd never offered it before."

ANDREA: "The poetry that you just spoke of, does it have pictures?"

DE ANGELI: "Yes, I think we would use little spots from the nursery rhymes and from various other books."

GREG: "Do you think you could tell us a little more about how Lapeer was, back...?"

DE ANGELI: "Well, I have pictures in my mind of what Nipsing Street was like, but maybe I said this before, didn't I? What Nipsing Street was like to my way of thinking. There was a bakery near Uncle Charley's store...Charley Tuttle...there aren't any Tuttles left, I guess. I noticed when I read your letters, there weren't any Turnbulls, nor any Tuttles, nor any Loffts, my father was a Lofft..."

TURNBULL: "...Nor any Lockwoods, nor Houghs..."

DE ANGELI: "I found a great many foreign names, some Polish names. Are any of you here who have Polish or foreign backgrounds? I have Polish friends and one of my books is **Up the Hill,** do you have that? **Up the Hill** is about Polish children and my friend, Edward Ryglewicz, helped me with that; there's a little glossary of the words, and how to say them."

TURNBULL: "You might tell them about your Grandfather Lofft."

DE ANGELI: "Oh, yes! Grandfather Lofft, my father's father had a--what would you call it?"

ANDERSON: "Blacksmith shop."

DE ANGELI: "Blacksmith shop, yes. And now the street is no longer there; it's been made into a little square in the center of town."

TURNBULL: "I think it would be on Fox Street, an extension of that. It would have been just north of the butcher shop. That's where the parking lot is."

Page 34

DE ANGELI: *"I loved to go there and watch him work, heat the iron in the fire and work with the bellows to get it hot...And beside that, he sang in the church, and I remember that after I'd been married, I was on my way west to meet my husband, who had gone ahead. So I was here for a visit at my grandmother's and I sang a duet with my grandfather and...tears ran down his cheeks, while we were singing!"*

DAVID: *"How long did it take you usually, to write one of the books?"*

DE ANGELI: *"Well, at least a year... now* **The Old Testament** *took me three years and the* **Nursery Rhymes**--*do any of you know the* **Nursery Rhymes?** *Well, that took me three and a half years, to gather the rhymes together. I knew about a hundred myself and then we had other books, so that I would have a pretty full collection. And then I illustrated them. You see, a full-page drawing, such as...let's see [showing a color two-page illustration in* **The Door in the Wall**]. *Now, that wouldn't perhaps take me a month, but one with figures in, that would take me at least a month to do. I used to do the writing first and then I would take it to New York to my editor at the Doubleday Company and at that time, Margaret Lesser was my editor; she was my editor for forty years and she would go over the story with me. We would divide it into the pages so that, she'd say, 'Now where do you want your pictures; how big do you think you want them on this page?' And we would decide that way. Then I'd go home and make the drawings. Sometimes it was a full page. And I was only allowed so many pages in color because color is very expensive to reproduce."*

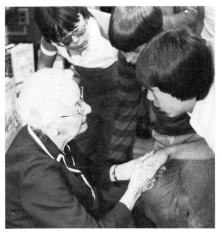

Visiting with David Churchill, Skip Le Por and Russell Arnold, at White Junior High.

ANDERSON: *"You first had to do what they call color separations."*

DE ANGELI: *"At first, in* **Henner's Lydia**; *I did color separations."*

ANDERSON: *"Such as the one with the jars of jelly?"*

DE ANGELI: *"Oh my yes, that was particularly hard to do... Well, because I was not known--my name was not known--when I did this, it was one of the first, after the Ted and Nina...two Ted and Nina books, when I did this. And they said, 'now you can do this book, if you will do the separations'. That means, you see when they do printing, they print one color, then they have a key to know exactly where to put down the next plate and then they print another color...black, red, yellow and blue. I had to make a drawing in pen and ink of this, first. Then I had to reverse it and draw that on the glass about twenty by thirty, I guess. They had to be exact size and my husband made a...put a piece of glass in my drawing board, my drawing table, so that I could see through the glass what I was doing and then I had to reverse that drawing I had made and do it backwards on this piece of glass. No, I've got that wrong. They photographed those drawings in reverse in light blue, which had no value of its own and I had to re-trace everything I wanted to stay on this glass. Have you ever worked on a glass slate? Well, we used to...and it was like that. This was frosted glass so you can use regular pencil, an ordinary soft pencil. And I had to re-trace every single line that I wanted to stay there. Then, in order to have a green dress, I had to put a certain amount of blue into a certain amount of yellow. And I couldn't tell for sure what that color would be and that's much more near what I wanted it, than what I would have dared to think...So it was very difficult to do; it was very tedious. And then there'd be maybe twenty drawings on this sheet of glass and it took me months and months. But, it came out fairly well. I was amazed that it came out that well."*

JOHN: *"Do you still do illustrations?"*

DE ANGELI: *"Yes, until I did my last book."*

ANDREA: *"When you were doing your later books, did you have to do it like that, on glass?"*

DE ANGELI: *"I only had to do the first three books that way; I think **Copper-Toed Boots,** was the last one I had to do that way. Then, after that, I painted them in color and they reproduced them, because my books were selling by then. See, this made it less expensive, because an engraver has to work on your drawings to make the colors of the same value."*

JOHN: *"When did you start your drawings?"*

DE ANGELI: *"Well, at home. You see, when I was still singing I was married; I had three children and then I met a neighbor who was an illustrator. I met him through his mother...she came over to tell me that he had signed a contract with the Hearst publications. 'OH!, I said--he's an illustrator; that's what I've wanted to do all my life. Can I meet him?' So, she arranged that I should have tea in the studio where this man worked and my husband took the children to the circus, so I would be free and I just walked on air, because this is what I had wanted to do all my life...So, he was so busy that he said he couldn't take me as a pupil but he said, if you're in earnest, I will give you criticism, which is what happened. So he told me to go home and draw something, to let him see what I could draw. So I drew a boy, thinking about a story my father used to tell, then I found it difficult to get hold of Mr. Bower, because he worked at night. So one day, he happened to be late going to work and I saw him over there, and I asked him to come over and see what I had done. And when he saw it, he said 'Oh! I see, you're in earnest. Well, now, let's talk about this. I suggest you give up your public singing, because that would be spreading yourself too thin.' So I gladly gave it up. Then he said, 'I want you to do three drawings...' And I think I said to myself, 'I must do something before I am thirty-five.' "*

SKIP: *"Did you plan to write books when you were young?"*

DE ANGELI: *"Well as I said, I'd wanted to do it all my life. Ever since I can remember. But I had other things to do first. But maybe it was all for the best, you see, because everything I had done, helped me with everything else. When I had the children, I found out how to draw children and I studied anatomy when I bathed them. Even their bones and how they connected and so forth..."*

ANDREA: *"When you were in high school, did you take art courses?"*

DE ANGELI: *"Yes, I did, but it wasn't very helpful in creating. I did have some drawing classes once a week. And I had German, French, Latin and botany..."*

JOHN: *"Do you speak foreign languages now?"*

DE ANGELI: *"No, but I have a <u>feeling</u> for language."*

TURNBULL: *"The first time I remember Marguerite was when she came as a bride to Lapeer and all my aunts and mother and grandmothers and so on, had a party for her...it was sort of a shower...and during the afternoon, she sketched a picture of everyone at the party..."*

Page 36

DE ANGELI: "Did I?..."

TURNBULL: "...And when the party was over, she had the sketch done. And her sister was also going to be married, so Nina came too...and that was the first time I remember seeing her. Of course she had been away for a while. And I thought that was SO wonderful, because those pictures actually looked like the people..."

DE ANGELI: [As she was preparing to leave the classroom] "Let me tell you something: I'M HAPPY! I've loved being here with you..."

"For a lady whose life has been devoted to children, and who has made such an impact on children's lives, what would our program today be without children involved?" asked librarian Bettie Koerber. Making presentations to Mrs. de Angeli at the dedication were Katy Liming and Frankie Burger.

VI. THE MARGUERITE DE ANGELI LIBRARY

For many years, Marguerite de Angeli's visits to Lapeer were events marked with parties, visiting, autographing and remembering, as local people grew to know their author more closely and appreciate her loveable characteristics. But her last visit to town in 1981 was the grandest of them all.

In 1981, Lapeer formally celebrated its sesquicentennial during the month of August. Organizers hoped to bring back 92 year old Marguerite de Angeli for some of the festivities. Marguerite, before getting her official summons, was hoping to visit Michigan anyway. In July she mentioned to this writer that "I had been thinking I might go to Lapeer for a week or so, but none of my cousins seem to be at home. Later, I am going to Maine..."

Excitement was great when Sam Moray of the Lapeer County Historical Society received word of the distinguished author's acceptance in participating with Lapeer's celebration. Wheels quickly were set in motion to celebrate Marguerite de Angeli once again. It was arranged that an exhibit of twenty-three original art works from *The Empty Barn* would be displayed in the historic Lapeer County Courthouse, where a permanent de Angeli showcase was already established. Marguerite was selected as grand marshall of the Lapeer Days parade; she would be given a key to the city and be the guest of honor at a VIP luncheon.

But most significant for her admirers seemed to be the August 6, 1981 resolution of the Lapeer County Library. The library board decided that effective August 22, 1981, "the Lapeer City Branch Library shall henceforth be known as the Marguerite de Angeli Branch Library."

Marguerite knew that she was to preside over Lapeer's celebration but not that the library-- and libraries seemed synonymous with her life-work--would be dedicated to her. The secret was carefully kept from her, even though excitement was great in Lapeer and among her family. As Jim Jessop of the Lapeer schools noted, "The greatest is the renaming of the library... how often does a person get a building named after them and how seldom during their lifetime?"

For Marguerite, the 1981 return home was undoubtedly the happiest. She first visited with her grandaughter Kate Creitz, who was Arthur's daughter and lived in Troy, Michigan. There she spent time with her two great-grandchildren Colin and Abby, and was especially pleased when her son Arthur and his wife Nina joined the family. And when she came to Lapeer, she again visited in the homes of her cousins Ruth Turnbull and Jean Harrison.

The summer morning of August 22 was among the best of the season when Marguerite and three generations of her family arrived on the library lawn. She was surprised at the crowd of hundreds who had gathered on the spacious grounds, but soon she realized: they had come to see her. Friends old and new greeted her, including perhaps the last of her childhood friends, Dorothy Davis, whom Marguerite still called "Little Dorothy."

The highlight of the dedication ceremony was the hanging of the new sign designating the library as the de Angeli Library. Marguerite was thrilled to see the sign and was touched as tributes were paid to her by Laura Strauss, Bettie Koerber and Phyllis Clark, librarians. Then she stood before the microphone to say, "I must tell you all that I don't know what I have ever done to deserve this, and I'm very happy, so happy I can't help crying. This is one of the happiest days of my life!"

For Marguerite, the day continued to be joyous. In an open car, she rode with her granddaughter Kate and Kate's two children down Nepessing Street as grand marshall of the parade. Applause frequently broke out as her car passed and once again she was reminded of her special spot in the hearts of Lapeer.

Still, Marguerite de Angeli was incredulous that all the honor had come to her. "I am quite humbled by having the library named for me!" she admitted.

The final return to Lapeer was a triumphant one.

The expanded Marguerite de Angeli Library.

The newly named Marguerite de Angeli Library had been opened in 1923, and was said to be the last of the Carnegie-financed libraries in the United States. Although it was architecturally pleasing, the facilities were far too small to serve the community. Plans were drawn up to modernize and add a major addition to the building, which was completed in 1984. The enlargement was enthusiastically supported by the Lapeer community. It was also a project which the de Angeli family watched with interest.

With Marguerite living in compact quarters at Cathedral Village in Philadelphia, her life-long accumulation of manuscripts, memorabilia, art work and honoraria was stored away in various homes of her children. The family, through Kate de Angeli Creitz, offered much of this treasured collection for display in the enlarged library in Lapeer. "This is the place where Grandma is loved and remembered," Kate noted. "The family all agrees that this collection belongs in the de Angeli Library where it can be seen and enjoyed."

When transported to the library in 1986, excitement was great when boxes were unpacked. Included were six book manuscripts, including *Friendship and Other Poems, The Empty Barn, Fiddlestrings, Whistle for the Crossing, The Door in the Wall: A Play*, and the Newbery winner, *The Door in the Wall*. Over 150 original illustrations came with the collection, representing Marguerite's work from the 1930s to the 1980s. Family photos and artifacts were also among the stacks of materials.

Representing Marguerite's many honors, the Newbery Medal and the Regina Award came to Lapeer for exhibition. Large citations from Villanova University and the Pennsylvania Library Association were among the treasure trove of artifacts.

"This is a literary collection that any library would be proud to have," noted librarian Laura Strauss. The memorabilia meant that Lapeer joined two other repositories with major collections of de Angeli material: The Free Library of Philadelphia and University of Minnesota's Kerlan Collection.

With the choice sampling of Marguerite's work came the responsibility of preserving it and displaying for the enjoyment of library patrons and scholars who wished to study the significant sampler of children's literature. Lapeer again responded with generosity in regard to its author. Service clubs, banks, the McDonald's management company, the Lapeer Fine Arts Council, the Lapeer Education Association and many individuals donated funds to enable display cases to be constructed.

Showcases at the de Angeli Library display the author's memorabilia and art.

Much of the newly arrived collection was premiered for the first time at the annual celebration of Marguerite de Angeli's birthday, held at the library on March 14, 1986. The library's new meeting room was selected as a site for the permanent display and showcases were crafted by Lapeer West High School teachers David Weisler and Richard Mayberry.

The Marguerite de Angeli exhibit was first arranged in June of 1986. The permanent tribute adds to previous displays in the library, including an oil portrait of their mother donated by the de Angelis, framed art from *Copper-Toed Boots* and a permanent collection of editions of the thirty books produced by Lapeer's most famous and favorite former resident.

Grand marshall of the Lapeer Days parade

Courtesy of The Flint Journal.

*Attending the annual March 14 party for Marguerite de Angeli in 1986, held at her namesake library in Lapeer, family members enjoy **The Empty Barn**. Reading to her six-year old daughter Abby is Kate de Angeli Creitz, granddaughter of Marguerite de Angeli.*

Marguerite, wearing her grand marshall badge, with Sarah, a young relative, in Lapeer.

Bettie Koerber presents a bouquet.

Marguerite with son Arthur and his wife Nina.

Meeting a girlhood friend, Dorothy Davis

The old sign comes down and the new sign for the de Angeli Library is hung.

About 1908 - Marguerite and her brothers.
Left to right: Arthur, Dick, Walter and Harry

Family Thanksgiving in front of Lofft home - Collingswood, N.J.
Top: Richard, Marguerite, (Maude Kreiger, a friend) Anna de Angeli (sister of Dai), Arthur and Alma Lofft,
Walter, Arthur de Angeli, Jack de Angeli.
Bottom: Knut Kreiger (son of Maude - above) Shad Lofft holding granddaughter Adelle, Ruby Lofft, Nina
de Angeli and Dai.

MARCH 14, 1981

This picture was taken at the Philadelphia Library.

Front row, left to right: Bonnie Walton (daughter of Adelle and Jack Walton), Marguerite, Debra Walls, great granddaughter of Marguerite, (daughter of Nina Walls).

2nd row: Edna de Angeli (wife of Jack), Betty de Angeli (Ted's wife), Marion (Maurie's wife), Nina (Arthur's wife), Adelle Walton (wife of John, niece of Marguerite), Ted de Angeli.

3rd row: William W. Walls (husband of Nina Walls), Maurice de Angeli, Nina de Angeli Walls (granddaughter), Jack de Angeli, Daniel de Angeli (son of Maurice), Arthur de Angeli, Jack de Angeli (son of Maurice), John H. Walton.

APPENDIX I

UNTOLD TALES FROM COPPER-TOED BOOTS

*In 1954, Hazel Emry of Central Michigan University solicited a number of Michigan-related authors for manuscript materials for a collection at the college. Marguerite de Angeli responded to Miss Emry's request, donating a working draft of **Copper-Toed Boots**, preliminary sketches, and a pasted-up dummy of the book. The material is now in the Clarke Historical Library at Central Michigan in Mt. Pleasant. "It pleases me that my books are of enough interest in Michigan for you to want the original manuscript," Marguerite wrote.*

*In 1971, Marguerite de Angeli donated another collection of rough drafts, pre-writing notes, sketches and manuscript material used in writing **Copper-Toed Boots** to the Lapeer County Historical Society on the occasion of the week-long festivities in the author's honor. This prized manuscript has been exhibited in Lapeer with a great deal of interest and pride.*

*In both of the **Copper-Toed Boots** drafts, story material which was not used in the final version of the book can be found. All this excess material, while not polished to final draft form, sheds facinating light on life in Lapeer in the 1870s. For that purpose, several extracts are printed here. Ed. note.*

FIRE IN THE FOURTH WARD

Clang! Clang! Clang!--Clang! Clang! Clang! Clang!-Shad sat up in bed with a start, and thought the house must be afire; the whole room was a red glare, the quilt was red, the slanted ceiling, and even the dark wood of the bureau looked red. He jumped out of bed, grabbed his trousers and ran to the window, calling as he went, "Will!, Will!, Will!"

The whole sky seemed to be ablaze. Will half opened his eyes.

"Will! Will!" called Shad again. "There's a fire! Get your pants on quick."

Will looked bewildered, but got out of bed and started putting on his trousers over his nightshirt. He was still so near asleep that he got them on backwards and had to change them. Clang! Clang! Clang! Clang! went the fire bell.

"Hurry! Hurry!" said Shad, buttoning his suspenders, as he went toward the stair well.

"Better put on our boots." said Will. "You know how Ma hates us to go barefoot. Besides there's likely to be sparks and things!"

Shad came back and both struggled into their boots, then dashed down the stairs, two at a time, putting on their coats as they went. It was late spring, but still cold at night.

They found Pa up too. He was putting on his boots. Ma was standing at the window in her long gown, her eyes starting out of her head. Ma didn't like fires. Shad and Will thought they were splendid.

Clang! Clang! Clang!---Then Clang! Clang! Clang!--There were hurried footsteps going by and excited voices.

"Must be the fourth ward," said Ma. "That's what <u>I</u> counted. There goes Elder Perkins. <u>Dear!</u> I hope they can get the engine out!" She was speaking to the empty air.

Pa, Will and Shad had gone. The door slammed and they were running down the street toward the firehouse. Ash caught up to them just at the next corner, then all calling excitedly to one another,

"Know where the fire is?"--

"Sounds like the fourth ward!"

"Wonder if Caleb has brought his horses yet?"

"Wonder what started it?"

The bell kept up a constant clamor, slowing at intervals to toll out the ward number. The sky was billiant red. Every now and then a shower of sparks would burst into the air, to be followed by a great roll of black smoke. It seemed to be so near that Shad thought it must be right on the main street, but Pa said,

"No, you'll find that's 'way over town somewhere."

When they reached the firehouse, it seemed as if every man and boy for miles around was standing on the walk before the closed doors, all talking at once, but no one seemed to be getting the engine out.

"What's the matter?" called Pa. "Hasn't Caleb come with his team? Where's Ed Miles, isn't he here either?"

"Ed's got chills and fever," said Philander. "Come down with it this afternoon. 'N Caleb's horses been down to that new farm of his, the last few days. He's gone to see if he can get Elgin's team.

They could hardly make themselves heard above the loud clang of the bell that Dan'l kept ringing as furiously as he could make it go.

"Want I should take Ed's place?" said Pa, and without waiting for an answer , he took the big key from Horace and opened the door. The fireman trooped in to get their helmets and rubber coats.

"Come on!" someone called, "Let's pull the engine out and get ready to go as soon as Caleb comes with the team. Come on!"

The boys swarmed in ahead of the men, pulling at the wagon tongue and dragging out the heavy engine.

"Look out now, you fellows!" called Pa, "or that engine will be too much for you on that slope!" But they were all so excited they paid no attention and dragged the engine out onto the road. Having once got started, they went faster and faster and before the boys knew what was happening, had started down the slope where the road ran into Nepessing Street.

She had broken loose entirely and was going at top speed. Shad and Will had tight hold of each other's hands, they were so excited Shad could hardly keep from laughing; everyone looked so funny sprawled along the road, so astonished they couldn't move. The air was filled with smoke but the sky was so bright that each face was bathed in a ruddy glow. For a moment they all sat there as if turned to stone, then one after another they jumped to their feet and ran, Philander first, next Pa and then all the others, racing down the dusty road. They grabbed the back wheels of the engine with all their might and tugged, but it was no use.

Faster and faster down the road she went, then struck a stone, swerved to one side, and suddenly stopped. No wonder! The wagon tongue was rammed at least six feet into the bank!

The tongue had gone into the bank with such force that all their efforts couldn't budge it. Then Caleb came with the team he had borrowed, saw the predicament they were in and began to find a way to hitch the horses to the back of the wagon.He muttered to himself

Page 45

about what stupid critters some folks were, and said, ''Now all you boys git out of the way!''

All this time, the bell kept ringing frantically, but the smoke was lessening and the glow was fading from the sky. The men struggled to help the horses free the engine from the mudbank, and finally succeeded. They then had to take the team, from the back of the wagon and hitch them to the front.

The last buckle was scarcely fastened before they were off in a gallop in the direction of the fire, with a stream of running men and boys following. It was only a few blocks down Nepessing Street but when they reached the spot, the roof was gone and what had been Varnum's Mill was just a smouldering ruin. Fortunately, it stood near the creek. The hose was soon thrust into the water and the men were up on the engine, pumping for dear life.

Suddenly a yell went up from the crowd. Right near where Shad and Will were standing the hose had burst and was showering everybody with a thick layer of mud. Frank Till and Ben Tuttle stood with mud dripping from their hands, from their chins and from the ends of their noses. Their clothes were covered from head to toe.

Shad had to cram his hand in his mouth to keep from laughing and Ash just rolled on the ground and laughed. There was so much going on that nobody took any notice of it.

The men stopped pumping while Caleb and Pa took out a section of hose. Meanwhile, the fire blazed on merrily. By the time the hose was fixed, there wasn't much left for the fire to burn, but the men started pumping again, and the muddy stream played on the charred beams. They kept at it until all the licking flames were gone and only a thick steamy smoke arose from the ground.

Pa straightened up, took off the big fireman's hat and wiped the sweat from his brow. He stood breathing hard for a moment

''Whew!'' he said, ''Poor management--poor, mighty poor!'' he shook his head.

''Horses ought to be kept here all the time, ready at hand. One time I remember, Tom Davis's barn was afire and the horses that were supposed to be used for the engine were 'way out two mile the other side of town, hitched to a threshing machine. Tom's own team was drawing lumber for his son's house, out by Columbiaville. Barn burned to the ground. Poor management, poor, mighty poor!''

All the excitement was gone. The crowd melted by twos and threes, except for one or two firemen who stayed to make sure that the fire didn't break out again. But the rest of the men and boys went back home to bed. Shad, Ash, Will and Steve walked back together over the bridge and up Nepessing Street. Shad thought how strange it looked at night with no lights in the windows and shutters closed. Not even Paris Evans' popcorn stand was lighted.

All was silence except for the quiet shuffling of their feet. They were too tired to talk. Steve said, ''Night''. Then in a few moments, Ash went his way and said ''Bye''. Shad and Will walked on and caught up to Pa.

The fire was over.

THE PINE SNAKE THAT CAME HOME WITH THE BERRIES

Early next morning, Ma loaded the spring wagon with a basket of food and pails for the boys to gather berries in. She covered the bottom of the wagon with an old quilt from the loft, and the boys and Sammy, the dog, piled in. Ma had said that Ash could go too, so he came with his dinner in a pail while they were still eating breakfast. Ma sat on the seat and let Cousin Lija drive as far as he went. The sun was very hot again; ''just right for berrying'' Ma said. Old Tom took his time about getting there, so the sun was high when Cousin Lija left them and they turned off the road. They found the patch thick with ripe fruit and a wild tangle of vines where an old saw mill had been deserted.

They hadn't been picking long when Ma said, "There must be a pine snake around here somewhere." She sniffed, "I smell it! And look at that dog, he smells it too!"

"Smell it?" said Ash.

"Yes, smell it!" said Ma. She sniffed again, and picked up a long stick to push back the bushes. The boys too, hunted all through the thicket, but found nothing. Sammy whimpered and sniffed but finally gave up looking.

The berries all hung so thick that it wasn't long till their pails were nearly filled and they stopped to eat.

"Up here under this old shed is a good place," said Shad. "Whew! it's hot!"

Ma sniffed again.

"I still think there is a pine snake here somewhere."

They searched again before sitting down, but as before, found nothing, so sat in the shade to eat and carried water to drink from the mill creek that ran clear and cool just below the hill. Back to picking berries they went, till every pail and basket was full to overflowing.

"Come now, youngsters," said Ma, "it's time to go. It must be four o'clock. Pa will be coming home and Old Tom doesn't like to hurry. Spread that quilt out a little and climb into the wagon. Shad whistled for Sammy.

When they reached home, Pa was there before them, and had the kettle on.

"Here, Will, you take these pails in. Ash, these are yours for your mother. Shad, said Ma, "You carry this old quilt up into the attic. Funny, I've smelled that snake all day. Imagination, I guess."

Shad gathered up the quilt and carried it up to the loft. He put it down on the floor, and was just going down the steps when the quilt moved! Shad's eyes popped out. He looked again. It moved again, and out of the torn place crept a pine snake at least four feet long! For a second, Shad looked in terror, then hastily let down the trap door and went running for Pa.

It was no trick at all for Pa to kill the snake. "But how did it get into the quilt?" Ma said, shuddering. "And why didn't we see that it was there? Well, no harm done, a miss is as good as a mile!"

JEFF DAVIS'S SADDLE

Shad wiggled closer to the warm chimney, the little chill in the spring air added to the delicious chill running down his spine as he read: "Over the bluff came the redskins, making the night horrible with their cries." He was sitting astride the roof peak with his back against the chimney where Pa and Ma would never think to look for him. It was Sunday afternoon, the heavy dinner was over, and Pa was probably asleep anyway.

If he hadn't been so absorbed in the "Nickel Library" he could have seen Ash coming around the corner. Ash looked very much dressed up, and very uncomfortable. He gave a low whistle, and as Shad looked up, motioned for him to come down. Shad tucked the nickel library in his coat and carefully worked his way to the edge of the low roof, dropped to the top of the shed and then to the ground. Not a word was spoken until the boys were around the corner on the way to Ash's house. Shad thought if he called attention to himself, Ma would be sure to want him for something. She would make him put on his necktie again, if nothing else.

"My folks have gone driving," said Ash. "There's nobody home but Grandpa. I didn't want to go. Nothing to see.''

Shad thought that if <u>he</u> had the chance to go driving behind Mr. Tomlinson's beautiful horses, he would go.

''What did your Pa say when he found out about our being sent home from school?'' Ash said. ''We can go back, you know. Pa talked to Father Busche when he came over for a book last night, and Father Busche talked to Miss McKinnon. She goes to his church, you know. So when Pa met her this morning on the street, she said she would give us another chance.

Shad was relieved. He wouldn't like to spend another year in the same grade. Shad was a little awed by Father Busche, but Ash, who saw him often, said he was good fun and was teaching him Latin. The Catholic church and the rectory were right across the road from the Tomlinson house. Back of the church was Catholic Hill, a fine place for coasting. Sometimes when Katy Brady, who kept house for Father Busche,* had been baking, she gave cakes to Ash. Ash said it wasn't true what some people said, that in the cellar of the rectory were all kinds of guns and things to start a revolution. He knew, because he had gone down there once to get a crock of butter for Katy. The cellar was just like any other cellar, filled with food, and wood piled neatly along the wall.

As the boys went into the arbor at Ash's house, on the way to the barn, they saw Father Busche walking up and down in his garden, reading his breviary. He did look kindly.

Just as they were starting up the ladder to the hayloft, Ash said: ''What do you say we go to Aunt Briggs'** to ride on the saddle?''

''What saddle'' Shad asked as he took out his Jew's harp and began twanging a tune.

''Jeff Davis's, of course,'' said Ash, getting down off the ladder. ''Where'd you get that Jew's harp? Give you my knife for it!''

Shad had hardly gotten used to having a Jew's harp, but he did want a knife. ''Take you!'' he said, wiping off the harp on his pants and handing it over. The knife was a beauty. Ash had gotten it for his birthday. It had four blades and a screw driver. He just had to open them all before he put it into his pocket. They went off down Calhoun Street toward Auntie Briggs' house.

''Aw come on!'' said Ash, trying to play ''John Brown's Body'' on the Jew's harp, and Shad humming it. He started to whistle it, then remembered it was Sunday, and abruptly stopped. Ma didn't like him to whistle on Sunday.

''What did you say about Jeff Davis?'' he asked. He thought Ash was just bragging. Ash took the Jew's harp out of his mouth so he could talk.

''I said my Auntie Briggs has his saddle, and she's got my Uncle Briggs's sword, too. The one he had in the war. I found it out the other day, and she's had 'em all this time. She said I could ride it any time I wanted to. Not really ride, of course, but on the sawhorse in the woodshed. She didn't say I could bring you, but if you get me some nails from your father's shop, maybe I could get her to let you play too.''

Ash didn't see any use in wasting a good opportunity. Nails, even horse shoe nails, came in handy.

''Oh, I guess I could,'' said Shad. Pa always had nails lying around that he wouldn't miss. ''Was it really Jeff Davis's saddle? How did your Uncle Briggs get it?'' It did not seem possible to Shad that anything belonging to so famous a person as Jeff Davis could be right here in Lapeer.

*Reverend John Busche, who served the Catholic church from 1864-1889.

**A ''Mrs. Briggs'' is shown as living on Court Street, in the block south of the Court House, in the 1874 Atlas of Lapeer.

They were going in the door at Auntie Briggs' house. Ash didn't have to knock, but walked right in and said to his aunt, who sat with a book in her lap,

''Hallo, Auntie, can Shad and I play with the saddle?'' He pulled Shad into the room. ''Look!'' he said, ''There's Uncle's sword, right over the mantle.''

Auntie Briggs was a pretty woman; she smiled pleasantly at Shad, who didn't know her very well. ''I guess you can,'' she said, putting her book down. ''But don't make too much noise.''

She opened a closet and took out the saddle. Shad eyed it with awe. To think that it had been in the war of rebellion! It had seen men killed, and the sword on the wall; it might have run through someone's body. Shad shivered just thinking about it.

Shad and his dog Sammy. An unpublished sketch by Marguerite de Angeli.

APPENDIX II

A MARGUERITE DE ANGELI BIBLIOGRAPHY

(All titles, unless indicated, were published by Doubleday Book Company)

Ted and Nina Go to the Grocery Store (1935)

After a decade of illustrating for other writers, de Angeli was asked by an editor to write and supply drawings for a small book suitable for first graders to read to themselves. ''There were Bettys and Peters everywhere,'' she noted, so she chose her own children's names for the principal characters. Her youngest son, Maury, was used as a model for the character of Ted. The subject matter for this book is simple and employs experiences familiar to most children.

Manuscript at Free Library of Philadelphia.

Ted and Nina Have a Happy Rainy Day (1936)

While the previous book was in progress, the author was asked to produce a companion title of the same genre, so that two books could be simultaneously printed, permitting Doubleday to sell each at 50ᶜ during the Depression economy. In the second book, the author described a day spent indoors out of the rain, exploring the trappings of the old attic.

The first two Ted and Nina books established the author's reputation and her connection with Doubleday, her major publisher, and Margaret Lesser, her only editor.

Henner's Lydia (1936)

This book describes life within an Amish family in the Pennsylvania Dutch country. With this book, de Angeli began her long tradition of on-the-scene research for authentic material and flavor. She spent time in the Amish country and through what she termed ''happy coincidences'' she was able to visit in the homes and schools of natives. Her editor once alluded to de Angeli's ''natural and unconscious friendliness which opened many a door to her.'' It was her enthusiastic spontaneity that helped her gain admission to Amish homes.

In 1978, the author remarked that *Henner's Lydia* was one of the best-selling of her long list of books.

Original manuscript and illustrations now at Kerlan Collection, University of Minnesota, hereafter cited as "Kerlan Collection".

Petite Suzanne (1937)

Because the French-Canadians, like the Pennsylvania Dutch, maintained their traditions, de Angeli was anxious to gather material and write of their culture. She journeyed to the Gaspe peninsula and lived with a French-Canadian family for a week. The result was a story filled with folkways and customs of daily life, as experienced by a French-Canadian girl named Suzanne.

Copper-Toed Boots (1938)

The book which Marguerite based on her own family and life in Lapeer, Michigan during the 1870s.

Manuscript and illustration in de Angeli collection in Lapeer, Michigan and at Central Michigan University.

Skippack School (1939)

Author Elsie Singmaster suggested that de Angeli examine the life of school-master and humanist Christopher Dock, who was legendary at the Mennonite School near Skippack, Pennsylvania during the 1700s. De Angeli conducted research for this book, which had as its protagonist a Mennonite boy named Eli Shrawder. Her use of the German Fractur Schriften adds to the decorative quality of this volume.

Original illustrations at Kerlan Collection; Manuscript at Free Library of Philadelphia.

A Summer Day with Ted and Nina (1940)

The third and last of the Ted and Nina series. All three books were re-issued under one cover in 1965 as *The Ted and Nina Storybook.*

Thee, Hannah! (1940)

In Moorestown, Pennsylvania, de Angeli was introduced to a 92-year old Quaker lady who became the prototype for the Hannah character. In this book, Quaker discipline and its effect on children was explored. The setting is Philadelphia in the 1850s and Abolitionists, Quakers and the Underground Railroad are described.

Original illustrations at Kerlan Collection; manuscript at Free Library of Philadelphia.

Elin's Amerika (1941)

This is the story of a Swedish settler who lived in Delaware at the time of William Penn. Kindly brotherhood and cooperation with the region's Indians are expressed in this story told through the point of view of Elin. De Angeli conducted research for this book at the Swedish Museum in South Philadelphia.

Original manuscript at Free Library of Philadelphia; illustrations in the Kerlan Collection.

Up the Hill (1942)

This book was born through the de Angelis' participation in musical quartets. Acquaintance with Mr. and Mrs. Edward Ryglewicz inspired this story of a young mine worker who aspires to an art career. De Angeli visited a Pennsylvania mining town and absorbed much local color. She also studied Polish customs, foods, language, music and daily life from her Polish friends. This book also provides a glossary and pronunciation key to words and phrases utilized in the text.

Yonie Wondernose (1944)

This is the second of de Angeli's books with the Pennsylvania Dutch country as a setting. It is another Amish family story, seen through the eyes of Yonie. In 1945, this book was a Caldecott Honor winner.
Manuscript and illustrations in Kerlan Collection.

Turkey for Christmas (1944)

This is one of two de Angeli titles which did not appear with Doubleday's imprint; it was issued by Westminster in 1944 as a small Christmas token. The story is the semi-autobiographical account, describing the Lofft family's first Christmas spent in Philadelphia after moving there in 1902. The first edition was decorated with small sketches, but in 1965, de Angeli provided a mixture of color and richly detailed charcoal sketches for a more lavish edition.
Manuscript at Free Library of Philadelphia; Drawings at de Angeli Library of Lapeer.

Bright April (1946)

This title is considered the first modern children's book about a black child. *Bright April* is set in the Germantown section of Philadelphia and was six years in the making before Doubleday would publish the story. In the story, de Angeli addresses the problem of racial prejudice and how children are able to gain understanding and tolerance through their own natural devices. *Bright April* was a milestone in children's publishing and stands out as an historic accomplishment in the field of children's literature.
An honor book of the New York Herald-Tribune's Spring Book Festival.
Manuscript at Free Library of Philadelphia; drawings at de Angeli Library of Lapeer.

Jared's Island (1947)

The de Angeli summer home at Tom's River, New Jersey suggested the setting for this book. The tale involves a Scottish boy named Jared Craig who shipwrecks on Barnagat Shoals in the early 1700's. He is rescued by a Quaker, but runs away to live with Indians. Rumors of Pirate legends in the de Angeli neighborhood of Money Island prompted the insertion of buried treasure within the plot-line. The symbol of a sentinel oak-tree which the author used in her story later proved to be a reality. "Once again," de Angeli noted, "I had imagined something that was true."
Manuscript at Free Library of Philadelphia; drawings at de Angeli Library of Lapeer.

The Door in the Wall (1949)

A crippled friend of the de Angeli family who participated with their musical evenings suggested to Marguerite the need for a book about a child dealing with a handicap. Robin, the hero of *The Door in The Wall*, struggles with his lameness in thirteenth century England. He is assisted in his search for self-worth by Brother Luke, a monk who tells him "It is better to have crooked legs than a crooked spirit." Robin, through his personal bravery, is able to save a beseiged castle, proving Brother Luke's advice to be true: "Thou hast only to follow the wall far enough and there will be a door in it." De Angeli remarked that she sought to show children in this story that: "It's not who you are that counts; it's what you do with what you have that matters."
The winner of the 1950 Newbery Award; given the Lewis Carroll Shelf Award in 1961.
Two manuscript drafts are at the de Angeli Library in Lapeer.

Just Like David (1951)

De Angeli explored "the curiously fascinating theme of the child's relationship to the outside world" in *Just Like David*. She used the family of her daughter Nina as prototypes for story and illustration, and the adventures of her grandsons, David, Henry and Jeffrey, as they moved from Pennsylvania to a new home near Cincinnati. In de Angeli's words, this book was "representative of most children's longing to be like an older brother or sister."

Book of Nursery and Mother Goose Rhymes (1954)

This is a lavish, oversized book, perennially successful and best-selling of the de Angeli books. Doubleday assigned its premiere author the task of illustrating and selecting this collection, which includes 376 rhymes. The project took three years to complete.

Haviland, in *Children and Literature: Views and Reviews*, considers this book "the best" and compliments de Angeli's "quick recognition of Mother Goose's go power. The pictures move and thanks to generously designed space, have ample room to bounce about. . ."

Full-page color illustrations are done in clean, soft pastels and reflect both the artist's familiarity with Philadelphia and London scenes. In illustrating a family around a holiday table, she combined Dickensan influence with her own Lofft family memories. Her granddaughter Kate (Arthur's daughter) served as a frequent model while the drawings were being made. Kate's personal copy of the book attests to her model status. Her grandmother wrote: "To Kate, who hops and skips through this book."

Arbuthnot, in *Children and Books*, praised the action which infused the art: ". . .Children and animals dance and prance across the pages. Little flowery bouquets and birds adorn the corners, and plump, pretty babies tumble here and there. . ."
A Caldecott Honor Book in 1955.
Original drawings in Kerlan Collection, Free Library of Philadelphia and de Angeli Library of Lapeer.

The Black Fox of Lorne (1956)

This book, which follows the Mother Goose volume, attests to de Angeli's versatility. *Black Fox of Lorne* is historical fiction for older readers and is comparable to *Door in*

the Wall in richness of historical setting. The story occurred in the tenth century, with two Viking twins shipwrecked on the Scottish coast. They seek to avenge the death of their father and encounter loyal clansmen at war, kindly shepherds, power-hungry lairds and staunch crofters. ''An ambitious novel,'' notes Kirkpatrick, ''atypical to the author's usual shorter stories of ordinary, day-to-day concerns.''
Newbery Honor Book, 1957.
Manuscript at Free Library of Philadelphia; illustrations in Kerlan Collection.

The Old Testament (1960)

Through her concertizing, de Angeli was familiar with the literature of the Old Testament and was interested in illustrating scenes from Biblical stories. Doubleday sent the author and her daughter Nina to the Holy Land to gather the local color and historical accuracy needed to illustrate this book with accurate flavor. The complete collection of the magnificent art produced by de Angeli for this oversized volume is at the Free Library of Philadelphia.

A Pocket Full of Posies (1961)

This is an abbreviated form of the original Mother Goose book, containing 77 of the most familiar jingles and a sampling of favorite illustrations from the previous work.

Marguerite de Angeli's Book of Favorite Hymns (1963)

This is an illustrated collection of favorite religious songs, many of them familiar to de Angeli from her musical career.

The Goose Girl (1964)

De Angeli's newly illustrated version of the Grimm favorite was from a new translation of the original story.
Manuscript at Free Library of Philadelphia.

The Empty Barn (1964)

Published by Westminster, this book was a collaboration between de Angeli and her son Arthur. It is a family story, involving Arthur's daughter Kate, and life in the Pennsylvania countryside.
Manuscript drafts, preliminary dummies and paste-ups and samplings of illustrations are at the de Angeli Library in Lapeer.

The Door in the Wall: A Play (1969)

A dramatization of the Newbery Award classic, which was written by Arthur de Angeli and illustrated by his mother.
Original manuscript drafts and preliminary publishing material are at the de Angeli Library in Lapeer.

Butter at the Old Price (1971)

This is Marguerite de Angeli's autobiography, chronicling her life and career through 1960. She traces her childhood in Lapeer and Philadelphia, her musical career, family life and beginnings as an illustrator. In detail she recounts all the interesting people, places, events and research which contributed to her literary career.
Original manuscript at Free Library of Philadelphia.

Fiddlestrings (1974)

This is one of de Angeli's longer books, based on the boyhood of her husband, John Dailey de Angeli, in the 1890s. De Angeli used as a sub-plot the difficulty of combining discipline of musical training with more active pursuits of boyhood. This book is in the vein of *Copper-Toed Boots* as it recounts the escapades of a family member.
Manuscript drafts at Free Library of Philadelphia and de Angeli Library of Lapeer; illustrations at de Angeli Library.

The Lion in the Box (1975)

This is the second of de Angeli's Christmas stories. "In essence, it is true," said the author. The tale is of a New York family, headed by a widowed mother who cleans offices for a living. The poverty of the family is especially evident around Christmas, when a huge crate arrives at their flat. Deliverymen tease the children by telling them a lion lives in the box. In fact, the box contained lavish gifts from wealthy Mrs. Stix, of the Stix, Baer and Fuller Department Store. An earlier meeting with Mama had prompted the rich woman's gifts.
Manuscript and assorted drawings at Free Library of Philadelphia.

Whistle for the Crossing (1975)

Early railroading forms the historical setting for this book published when the author was 88. The main character is Eddie, whose father is an engineer on the Camden and Amboy railroad. The engineer is chosen to make the first train run on new tracks from Philadelphia west to Pittsburg.
Manuscript versions at Free Library of Philadelphia and de Angeli Library; illustrations at de Angeli.

Friendship and Other Poems (1981)

This is a collection of poetry penned by Marguerite de Angeli over many years. It is a touching and fitting collection to finalize the monumental body of the author-illustrator's work. In her poems, de Angeli encompasses universally shared experiences from birth to death. She writes of childhood, marriage, parenting, grandparenting, friendship, separation, and ultimate "Transcendence". Her own rich life-experiences also inspire topics, including "London", "May in Michigan", majestic "October Day" and simple marvel of "Tent Worms".

De Angeli's poetry reflects her unflagging optimism, her heightened degree of innate humanity and the *joie de vivre* that sparks her writing. Her lifelong commitment to children is perhaps summed up in the lines:

'. . .*And friendship from the lovely child,*
An instant love. 'Twill never die.''

The book that began the career.

*A de Angeli illustration in the June, 1932 issue of **The Country Gentleman**. During the '30's, Marguerite was a steady contributor to the prestigious Curtis publication. Stylized drawings like this were put aside in later years in favor of her timeless representations of childhood in her books.*

Page 57

"The Couch of Deer", illustration for Elizabeth Coatworth's **Made in America**. *"Pay Mrs. de Angeli"* is written on the reverse of this pen-and-ink. Her commissions during the Depression were important income for the family.*

*Illustration from **Jared's Island**.*

ABOUT THE AUTHOR

William Anderson was an elementary student in Flint, Michigan when he was first introduced to the works of Marguerite de Angeli through **Copper-Toed Boots** *and* **The Door in the Wall.** *Later, while a teacher at White Junior High School in Lapeer, his class successfully petitioned Michigan governor William Milliken to proclaim Marguerite de Angeli Day in the State of Michigan on the author's ninetieth birthday.*

A graduate of Albion College, with Honors in English, and from South Dakota State University with an M.A. in English, he is interested in history and literature. He has written numerous books and articles, and contributes regularly to **Travel and Leisure, American History Illustrated, The Saturday Evening Post, The American West** *and other magazines. For children, he has written for* **Highlights, Cobblestone,** *and* **Jack and Jill.**

The recipient of several awards for historical research and writing, he frequently participates at writing conferences, historical and children's literature festivals throughout the United States.